The History of
Radley Church of England School

by

Christine Wootton

Published by Radley History Club 2008
www.communigate.co.uk/oxford/radleyhistoryclub

Cover: grant.hilditch@enso.freeserve.co.uk

ISBN 978-0-9542761-5-7

Printed and bound by

Parchments of Oxford
Printworks, Crescent Road, Oxford, England OX4 2PB
email: print@parchmentUK.com   www.ParchmentUK.com

Contents

Introduction

When I volunteered to edit a booklet about Radley School in connection with Radley History Club's project, *Radley School - Then and Now*, there appeared to be very little material available and it seemed that the booklet would mainly consist of reminiscences from people whom we knew had been connected with the school. However, to the great delight of the History Club, the log books dating from 1866 to modern times were discovered. These provided a wealth of information and the idea of writing a small booklet changed into writing a book, with my own role expanded from editor to author. Many people have assisted me in this work and I am very grateful to them.

It was a very enjoyable experience immersing myself in the past life of the school and I have been able to discover a little of what it was like to live in Radley in days gone by. The log books brought back many memories for me as the school I attended as a child, and later taught at, retained many of its Victorian characteristics. I began my own education sitting at an iron-framed double wooden desk using a small slate/blackboard and chalk, as paper was scarce at the end of World War II. When I finished my career as a teacher, we were using computers and electronic white boards. Progress was rapid in the second half of the last century and the history of Radley school reflects this. It was fascinating to observe how fashions in education came and went and sometimes came round again.

In this book I have tried to cater for people's varied interests. For those interested in the history of education I have included the various Acts of Parliament, which radically changed the lives of children. At the end of the book, there is extra information about these Acts, which Stanley Baker, Radley History Club's archivist, contributed. For readers interested in social history there are items reflecting the changing times. For those who have attended the school, or whose ancestors have attended, I have included interesting events, information about the children and a reminder of what the curriculum, staffing, buildings and relationships with the church were like through the years. I hope that everyone will find something of interest and that it will bring back happy memories to former pupils. Chapters 2 to 9 are arranged in chronological order, which enables the book to be read as a whole or in separate sections of particular interest to the reader.

Most of the information has been taken from the school log books but the Radley parish magazines, *Radley News*, the Berkshire and Oxfordshire record offices and the Internet have been valuable sources too. Past and present pupils, parents, teachers and friends of the school have been very generous in giving their reminiscences and this has been a great help to me.

I do apologise if I have made mistakes, especially with the names and dates of people who worked at the school. I could only use what information I found, which means that there are quite likely to be some staff and items of interest missed out.

This book is dedicated to past and present pupils, parents, friends and staff of Radley Church of England School. They are the people who have made the history of this village school so interesting.

Christine Wootton

April 2008.

Acknowledgements

I am very grateful to the following people and organizations, especially the first two:

Stanley Baker, Radley History Club's archivist, for his very helpful advice, encouragement and support, especially on historical matters, for contributing the 'History of Education' section and for writing about the book on the back cover. I am also most grateful to him for his careful proofreading as the book progressed through the various stages.

Patrick Dockar-Drysdale for his painstaking proofreading, especially of the final document and for offering suggestions about the layout of the book. I could not resist making amendments to the book after Paddy had edited it, which means that any mistakes that are found are probably mine.

The project sub-committee of Radley History Club, who between them conducted interviews, collected information, read the first drafts of the book, helped with plans of the school and generally supported me in many different ways.

Ann Blake.
Eric Blanks.
Rita and Brian Ford.

Malcolm Grieve.
John Homewood.
Tony Rogerson.

For agreeing to be interviewed by Radley History Club.

Louise Beaumont.
Radka Benton.
Anne Blundell.
Beryl and David Buckle.
Jenny Davie.
Alison Grimes.
Dot Hewlett.
Don Jones.
Ray Osborne.

Rosalind Murdoch.
Mick Portsmouth.
Mary Shayler.
Roger Stephens.
Charlie Steptoe.
Brian Talboys.
Linda Thomas.
Ann Thorp.
Marjorie Whiting.

For help and/or photographs.

Maureen and Derek Cook.   Freda Faulkner.
Nicola Jenkins   Frances Lockwood.
Doug Rawlinson.   Joan Sharples.
Caryline Warner.

The late Ethel Lay's recollections given to the History Club by her niece
Maureen Holland.

Members of Radley History Club.

Harry Burton, Alice Cook, Thomas Harris, Bethan Long, and Mrs. Claire
Burton who helped me to take measurements of the old school and showed me
around the newer part.

Oxfordshire County Council Photographic Archive.
Berkshire Record Office.
Kelly's Directories at Abingdon Library.
The National Society, Bermondsey, London.
Radley News.
Radley C E School web site.
Radley College Archive Centre.
Wikipedia, the free Internet encyclopedia.
Oxford Local History Library.
The Times Educational Supplement.
The *Oxford Times* and *Oxford Mail.*

My grateful thanks go to Grant Hilditch, who kindly designed the front cover of this book
and to Radley Parish Council who gave a grant towards the production costs.

I sincerely hope nobody has been missed out and I do apologise if this is the case.

Chapter 1

Radley School buildings from about 1841 to 2007

The condition of the school is not satisfactory, nor indeed can it be in the present state of the premises. The existing buildings are inconvenient and ill adapted for the purpose of a school. They are also badly placed being three quarters of a mile from the bulk of the population. The managers should be urged to erect suitable buildings at a convenient spot. Unless this be done, the teacher's efforts to educate the children can under the most favourable circumstances be but partially successful.

The above was a summary of the report by Her Majesty's Inspector of Schools (HMI) after his examination of Radley Church of England School in November 1866. The floor of the school was of brick and the desks for the children were against the wall. The rain was coming in through a broken window and the chimney caused smoke to enter the classroom when a fire was lit. The teacher sometimes had problems lighting the fire in the first place, as the faggots were often damp. Consequently in winter the school often managed without a fire.

It has not been possible to establish how long a school in Radley had been in existence by the time the above report was written. At the 1851 census a man by the name of John Palmer had his occupation described as a schoolmaster. He was born in Radley and was also a resident there in 1841, which is the date when some people think the school house was built. In that year the School Sites Act 1841 permitted owners of land to convey not more than one acre for the site of a school, for the education of poor persons or for the residence of a school master or mistress. A reversion clause provided for such land to revert to the original owner or his successors if it ceased to be used for the purposes stated in the Act. Many schools were built under these provisions and it seems likely that at about this time Sir George Bowyer, 2nd Baronet of Radley, owner of Radley Hall and most of the land in the surrounding area, made available a small section of his land adjoining Radley Church for a school house and school. As early as 1833 it had been possible to obtain a grant from the Government for the construction of schools for poor children but it is not known whether Radley received one. If it had been received, it would have meant that half the cost of the school would have had to be raised by private subscription.

In a religious census return of 1852, the vicar, either the Rev. William Beadon Heathcote or the Rev. John Radcliffe, wrote that there had been a Sunday school belonging to the

Established Church in Radley since 1807. It was held in a separate building near the church and there were 40 scholars, none of whom paid or provided their own books. Twelve of these children were attending a day school in 1852. At the Sunday school, where only reading and religious knowledge were taught, there were three unpaid female teachers and one paid male teacher.

In 1859, according to the parish records, Annie Laurie, daughter of John Robinson, was baptised in Radley and her father is described as the parish school master. The 1861 census informs us that Thomas Emerton was the school master in that year and Kelly's Directory for 1864 shows that he was still the head teacher then. At that time the Rev. Robert Gibbings was the incumbent of the parish church.

The inspector could not find any improvement in the school buildings at the inspection in 1867, when the Rev. W. H. Ranken was the vicar. His report showed that the school was in the same unsatisfactory state. Dimensions were given for the school room in the log book and are as follows:

<u>September 1869</u>

Length 38' 9"
Width   14' 4"
Height 14' 2"

January 1868 brought some hope when the vicar, the Rev. W. Wood, and Sir George Bowyer's agent visited the school to inform the head teacher that they were trying to acquire land for a new school. The managers also arranged for a new closet for the girls, with a shrubbery planted around it.

Some repairs were carried out in the school during the summer holidays of 1868, and the floor was washed. The turret on the school had been repaired earlier but it still leaked badly during a thunderstorm in April. In December of that year the inspector was again very disappointed by the lack of progress, although he realised the managers were still in treaty for a fresh site to erect suitable buildings. Each year the school was given a grant from their lordships at the Privy Council Office but on this occasion they lost one tenth of it because of poor examination results and poor buildings. The school was threatened that they would forfeit more money the following year unless something was done in the way of improvements. Nothing was done and, as a result of the poor examination results for 1869, the grant was reduced by two tenths. Some indication must have been given in a letter that progress was being made about a new school as the grant for the previous year was later paid.

The known grants for other years, showing how the payment-by-results system caused a great fluctuation in income, are as follows:

1873	£ 8 . 4 . 8
1874	£ 7 . 16 . 0
1875	£10 . 19 . 7
1876	£11 . 18 . 0
1878	£28 . 4 . 0
1879	£24 . 8 . 0
1880	£30 . 11 . 0
1884	£34 . 5 . 4
1885	£28 . 18 . 0

The entries in the log books for 1870 and 1871, during the colder parts of the year, showed some of the frustration the head teachers experienced with the smoky fire, particularly if the east wind were blowing. At times the school had to be closed and at other times the occupants managed without heating. The plaster of the school room needed repairing and the bell came out of its bearing, fortunately not while a child was nearby. The inspector reported in June that the condition of the school was very imperfect.

On 3rd May 1872, Sir George Bowyer, under the provisions of the School Sites Acts of 1841 and 1844, granted the vicar and church wardens a 99-year lease of the land and buildings next to the church, together with an adjoining piece of land containing 20½ poles at a rent of £1 . 6s per year, payable on June 24th and December 31st. The property had to be held upon trust to be used towards the education of the poorer class in Radley and to be conducted upon the principles of the National Society for Promoting the Education of the Poor in the Principles of the Established Church. The Church of England Record Office in London has a file dated 1872 - 1996, which includes information about various grant applications submitted by Radley C of E School to the National Society towards the cost of improving the school premises. In 1872 the society gave them a grant of £32. The National Society was founded in 1811 and set out to provide a church school, known as a national school in every parish in England and Wales. A statement made at the time recorded that:

> The National Religion should be made the foundation of National Education, and should be the first and chief thing taught to the poor, according to the excellent Liturgy and Catechism provided by our church.

Some years later, in January 1903, the Rev. Charles Boxall Longland wrote a letter to Mr. Simpkinson of Radley College and referred to the knowledge he had about the school's connection with Sir George Bowyer. It read:

Under Bishop Gore's institution here as vicar in 1893 this was a donative living and therefore the freehold of the vicarage and ground remained with the patron. Twenty years before Gore came, our present school was built in what had been the vicar's orchard with the consent of Sir George Bowyer. When the Bowyer property was sold, the College became the Patron of the living and offered it to Gore. He consented to accept it on consideration that he was instituted by the Bishop of the Diocese and thus this ceased to be a donative vicarage.

After a gap of six months with no entries in the log books a new school opened on 13th January 1873. It is not known whether the children had any form of schooling during the time when no entries were made but the school cash account book for 1872 showed that a Miss Miller had been paid a salary of £2 . 10 . 0 for the month of December. The new building had walls varying in thickness from 9" in some parts to 4½" in others. Evidence of a previous building on the same site comes from the chimney which was shared between the school and the school house. It is built in exactly the same style as the other school house chimney and there are the remains of it in the partitioned section of the old building, behind a cupboard backing on to the school house wall. When the new school building was constructed, chimneys were built on the south side in a different style. At present there is no evidence to show whether the old building was parallel with the school house or at right angles to it. There is a suggested plan for the new building in the Berkshire Record Office in Reading, drawn by the architect Edwin Dolby in about 1871. This plan, which can be seen in Radley History Club's 2002 publication *The History of Radley*, was submitted to the Warden at Radley College and must have formed the basis for a discussion about the new building. Although the dimensions do not match the one that was built there are some similarities. Radley College archives have a map dated 1884 which shows the village school. There appears to be an attached building, probably a coal-house, at the rear of the school, which seems similar to Dolby's original plan. Edwin Dolby was paid £20 for his work in designing the school. Accompanying Dolby's plan was a letter which read:

Abingdon, 6th August 1871,
The Rev. the Warden
St. Peter's College,
Radley.

Dear Sir,

I beg to hand you a rough little sketch of such a school as I think you require for Radley. I propose it should be erected of the local stone and covered with plain red tiles, and although there is no agreement whatever about it yet, I think it would not look badly. In making the drawing I have endeavoured to design it in such a way as that the cost may not exceed £250 and if the handling of stone materials be given I feel convinced the buildings will not exceed that sum.

The actual cost of levelling the ground and fencing are matters which I could not speak definitely about unless I saw the site but below £25 to £30 would be very adequate for that purpose.

In the event of your deciding upon the accompanying sketch it could of course be arranged with further drawings.

I am, dear Sir, Yours, very faithfully,

Edwin Dolby.

Edwin Dolby and his wife Emma were in residence in Albert Park, Abingdon, in 1871 and 1881 and the censuses of those dates describe him as a practising architect and surveyor. Bryans built the school and they received £329 . 3 . 4 for their work. Richard Bryan, born in Deptford, Kent, employed eight men in 1871 and lived in Railway Terrace, near Stert Street in Abingdon. By 1881 he was a clerk of works and was living near Halifax in Yorkshire.

The inspector was much happier in December 1873. He reported that the new room seemed to be a good, useful one, but it lacked a gallery for the infants, who were sitting upon benches with their feet dangling about. The gallery was erected the following month. In the 19th century Samuel Wilderspin, a pioneer in infant education, designed the '9 to 10 step gallery' for infant classrooms' and his idea spread throughout the country by the end of the century. The gallery allowed the children to see and be seen. In 1876 a curtain was put up to separate the infants from the juniors whilst at their lessons. Two years later curtains were put up at the windows to provide some shade. The gallery survived until April 1915 when it was pulled down. The inspector was then stating, 'The removal of the gallery in the infants' room would effect a vast improvement in the teaching conditions there'. It had obviously gone out of fashion as a teaching aid.

The new chimney caused almost as much smoke in the classroom as the old one and at times the children had to go outside to avoid it. The ventilators in the windows were of no use whatsoever and the teacher complained that the children were less energetic because of the stuffiness of the room. The HMI in 1887 reported that the school was good but the upper lights of the windows should open.

An open fire in the classroom, using coal or wood, was the means of heating, although not an ideal one, unfortunately. On one occasion two boys were punished for leaving the blackboard in front of the fire after putting it there to make the fire burn up better. They had gone out and the blackboard became rather burnt. A far sadder occasion occurred on 17th November 1887 when Edith Palmer of Standard VI was eating her dinner near the fire. Her

11

dress caught on fire and she was terribly burnt. She went round to the head teacher's house one mass of flames. With the assistance of William East the head teacher managed to extinguish the flames and Edith was shortly afterwards taken to the hospital in Abingdon, where she died three days later. There was an inquest and the coroner decided that there was not sufficient protection against accidents. He communicated with the managers about the subject and very soon afterwards fireguards were fitted. Edith was buried at Radley and all the children attended the funeral.

The building of the new school does not seem to have been of the highest standard as the head teacher was complaining in July 1888 of neuralgia caused by the poor state of the walls and roof of the school. During periods of excessive rain, water had free access into the school and dropped in various pools on the floor. Six months later, the Rev. J.W.Kempe, Curate of Radley, found everything satisfactory inside the school but the state of the playground was disgraceful. At about the same time the inspector informed the managers that the offices (toilets) for the girls should be separate from those for the teacher's house. There is no mention of toilets for the boys and an expert on toilets throughout history thought that the boys would just use the nearby field. Proper offices were built at the beginning of 1891, but the inspector was worried that there was a gate in the wooden fence which was not shewn on the approved plan. He said that it must be kept locked except when it was necessary to bring in coal. This gate probably separated the boys' playground from the offices. The following map shows the position of the school in 1888.

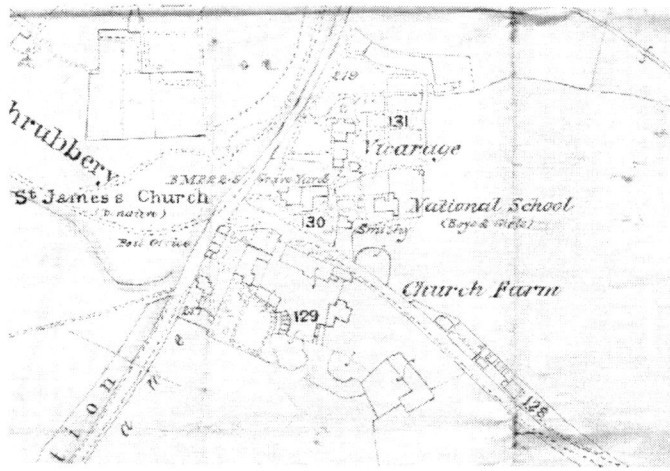

Map showing the school in Radley 1888.

By 1890 it became obvious that the infants ought to have a classroom of their own and the school prepared an entertainment in November of that year with proceeds going towards a new room. The 1891 inspection report endorsed the need for it and also said that another teacher was required for the younger children. It was about this time that the school became

12

a free one and parents no longer had to pay fees. The managers hoped that any fees already paid would be put towards a subscription to the building fund. During the 1891 Christmas holidays the porch was moved to the other end of the building and, at the beginning of 1892, an infant classroom costing £100 . 7 . 9 was built on the end of the school room. There was a sliding door to separate the new classroom from the old one. In April 1894 the following dimensions were given in the log book:

School room		Infants
Length	30'	18'
Wide	18'	16'
High	11½' to collar beam	12½' to collar beam

There was a platform in the infant room which the teacher later found to be in the way and suggested it be removed.

The infant classroom on the right was built in 1892.

By September 1893 the head teacher was having to draw to the attention of the vicar, the Rev. Charles Gore, the insecure state of the classroom. Builders were sent for and began work at once. Three months later a large portion of the ceiling fell down.

During the 1895 summer holidays the school walls were lime washed, the playground mended and strengthened and a lavatory was built on the south side of the school. This was the small building attached to the school near the school house and would only have had a washbasin in it. This extension is shown on an 1897 plan of the school. The *Parish Magazine* records that the manager, Mr. Simpkinson, donated £1 towards the building of the lavatory. The vicar, the Rev. James Okey Nash, wrote that it was like a small summer house and he hoped it would be no disfigurement to the school.

The summer of 1897 brought a change to the ownership of the school and its land and this was recorded by the vicar in the *Parish Magazine* of October 1897:

MISS BOWYER'S GIFT TO THE CHURCH AND SCHOOL

9th August 1897.

At long last a long-felt need is satisfied, and a long negotiation concluded, and Radley Parish owes Miss Mary Bowyer its sincere gratitude.

For a long time past the churchwardens have been obliged to answer their annual questions with 'insufficient' as regards the burial ground. Of course the churchyard has been in use for hundreds of years. Fathers and forefathers of our hamlet lie there for generations back. At last, however, it is settled. Mr. Richard Badcock has been unwearied in his patience over this matter in his desire to do a service to Radley, and has come over again and again to look over the land with the clergy, lawyers, and surveyors. The conclusion is that Miss Bowyer has freely given us the whole piece of land on which the school stands. The part on which the school stands is conveyed to the vicar and churchwardens under the School Sites Act (1841 and 1844), whereby the school and land become secured to us. The rest, including the forge and the approach to it, is conveyed to the vicar for the enlargement of the churchyard, under the Consecration of Churchyards Act (1867). All of us will desire to give our hearty thanks to Miss Bowyer for this act of consideration and generosity to the old home of her family. The village needs also to thank Messrs. Freshfields & Williams, the well-known solicitors, who out of goodwill have practically done the work for us for nothing - though in other ways there has been a good deal of legal expenses - and their knowledge of Radley circumstances has been very valuable. It is a satisfaction to know that the school is now secured, and that we have room to lay our dead to rest in peace.

Mary Bowyer, Sir George Bowyer's successor, was in Florence, Italy, at the time this conveyance took place. The new burial ground was consecrated in December 1897 and the children at the school received a half-day's holiday. The School Sites Act 1841, previously described, played an important role in this transaction. The school had to be under the management control of the vicar and a committee not exceeding six managers.

In the summer holidays of 1897 the school house had some renovation and one side of it was weather-tiled. The Rev. James Okey Nash, vicar of Radley from 1895 to 1898, hoped this would keep it dry.

In 1898 the HMI report on the school was far more satisfactory. The inspector suggested that the desks on the floor of the room should be removed and the gallery ought to be restructured and fitted with hinged desks. An excellent gallery, he said, had been erected in the infants' room but it was not quite big enough for all the infants. He thought one or two small desks ought to be provided for the babies. During the summer of 1898 the school had been thoroughly cleaned and painted. Unfortunately other problems were revealed.

The vicar, the Rev. Charles Boxall Longland, wrote:

> Alas! The paint-brush made sad discoveries. All the window frames of the school and house were entirely rotted away. One could push one's finger through them. So we have had to have new frames made, and many other repairs. This will cost a very great deal but we feel sure all who can will help us find the money for we are all proud of our school. Any contributions towards this unexpected though necessary outlay will be thankfully received by the treasurer at the vicarage.

The following month he wrote:

> Our first thoughts naturally turn this month to our school, about which we have heard so much in the way of begging - by a circular letter during the week - by the special pleading on Sunday last. This is what we have got to say about them, all the necessary repairs mentioned in our last month's issue have been completed. The only thing left now to be done is to pay the bills, which amount to just under £20. Towards this sum we have received subscriptions from Dr. Monk £2, Mrs. Bryans £1, the vicar, the Rev. Charles Longland, and Mrs. Longland, £1 . 10 to the amount of £4 . 10 . 0. Our collections on Sunday came to £3 . 12 . 3½ giving a total of £8 . 2 . 3½, leaving £12 still to be found before Christmas. We therefore hope that other gifts, however small, will quickly find their way to the school treasury, at the vicarage, to help complete the repair fund. Those of us who heard the Warden's excellent sermon on Sunday evening must have gathered many weighty reasons why we should all put our shoulders to the work of supporting and well equipping our village school. It is because we believe all the Articles of the Christian Faith. It is because by their Holy Baptism we have definitely pledged our children to the service of Christ their Lord that we, at all costs, will maintain the education which first, and above all

else, teaches us our duty towards our God. For in this manner alone can the true foundations of a noble character be laid and the honest and upright discharge of every after duty of life prepared for. If we really value these blessings ourselves, we surely shall always be ready to assist the work of our church school to the utmost of our means.

Some other donations came in, including one from Mrs. Woodley who gave one shilling. The debt was finally paid off in January 1899.

The 1901 report noted that the west end of the school adjoining the house was very badly lighted and that the insertion of a window in the north wall would be beneficial. The inspector was even more pleased in 1902 when he realised that, recently, money had been spent on the fabric of the school and that the window was about to be inserted.

It was in 1902 that the Balfour Education Act came into being. As a result of this Act the state took over responsibility for the education of eligible children and formed about 300 Local Education Authorities (LEAs). Funding came from taxation, which meant that it was an important first step in the provision of a state-provided, national, education system. It also meant that there would be some uniformity in educational provision throughout the country. It was, however, a very controversial Act as it set Anglicans against nonconformists in some areas. The reforms meant that church schools could receive their funding from the rates yet still retain their distinctive denominational status. The nonconformists were opposed to this and wanted the religious dimension in schools to be unbiased. Some people were upset by having large rate increases to fund children's education. This Act caused much anxiety for the managers of Radley School as they feared that it would lose its Church of England status. The problem arose because the school had not been defined as a church school when Miss Bowyer gave the lease of the land to the vicar and church wardens. Mr. Chandler of the National Society said that Miss Bowyer's deed was a very poor one and the lawyers ought to have known better. They had made no mention in it that the teaching of religion should be in the hands of the vicar. In fact, he went as far as to say that 'once a deed always a deed' and that the managers would 'just have to make the best of it'.

The Rev. Charles Longland in his letter of January 1903, previously referred to, continued:

> But there being some doubt as to the ownership of the school site - Miss Bowyer's lawyers were written to as she then owned the Bowyer estate and they in order to secure the ground for the purposes of the church school built upon it advised a Deed of Gift be drawn up and the property freely conveyed legally to the vicar and church wardens thereby intending to secure it as a church school.

16

But as the school then was and had been recognised as a church school I suppose neither they (the lawyers) nor the then vicar ever thought that the Deed of Conveyance of the site need describe exactly the method of religious teaching which is desirable in a church school. Hence no mention of necessary details is made in it.

From the letter of the Secretary of the National Society it seems now as if our only chance is this:

1. Will the Board of Education give us the power so far to amend our short Deed of Conveyance as to bring it into agreement with the National Society's Model Form, i.e. appeal to the Bishop?

2. The head teacher to be a bona fide member of the church and so too the foundation managers and that the vicar should be an 'ex officio' manager.

Could you find out if such a course is open to us or must we just slide under the Act as a 'Public Elementary School'?

The National Society's letter advised the school to use their 'Model Form' and included the information that if the vicar became an ex-officio member he would not personally be liable for repairs and the like.

Mr. Simpkinson's reply was too difficult to read. His entries in the school log books were almost impossible to read but this letter was worse.

The Rev. Longland then contacted the solicitors, Ellis, Bickersteth and Ellis of London and they, although not claiming to be experts in this type of law, concluded that the school seemed sufficiently protected. They wrote that the vicar would still be able to teach, particularly the catechism, and religious teaching would be in accordance with the Church of England. The solicitors also added that under the 1841 Education Act it was not allowed to convey the school property to a third party. The solicitors felt that there was no doubt that Radley was a denominational school.

Proof that the school was connected to the National Society came on 6th February 1903 when a letter to an unknown person showed that there was a deed between the two in 1872. It read:

Dear Sir,

You are right a grant of £32 was made in 1872.
£2 . 10 . 0 in 1878 -9
£1 . 10 . 0 in 1893.
There is a deed dated 29 July 1872.

Yours

F. J. Chandler. (Secretary of the National Society).

Further proof of the right to call the school a national school came in a letter dated February 9th 1903 from the National Society:

> Yes the 1872 Deed contains the National Society's [indecipherable] clause; that the school is certainly a National School.

> I should write to the Secretary to whom you sent EA2 and ask him to insert the fact or make an additional return if you have not made one for the school as yet.

> F. J. Chandler.

Questions about the Deed of Gift, etc. seemed to continue into 1906 when a letter to the Rev. Longland from an unknown person in Chester gave some explanation about the problems. It included:

> Chester.

> March 19th 1906

> The whole school was built in 1872-3 but I can't recollect what the cost was. There are no papers to give the information. The Rev. Charles Martin at Dartington Rectory might know. The impression was that they paid Sir George Bowyer 26/- a year for the school and got £5 in subscription from him.

> When the school was built I imagine some deed (perhaps a lease) was executed which secured the school for the purposes for which it was built and the Deed of Gift you refer to was to take the place of such a lease.

Charles Martin wrote in March 1906 with the same figures that are quoted earlier in this chapter. Some of the school's cash account books of the late 19th century indicate that £1 . 6 . 0 per annum was paid to Sir George Bowyer for the rent of the school house and school. The subscription from him averaged about £5. He showed interest in the school when he paid a visit one afternoon in November 1877.

As the number of children at the school increased, the head teacher, in 1903, started to ask for additional cloakroom accommodation. A new porch was eventually provided in September 1905 at a cost of £47 . 18 . 0 and at the same time a new window was installed. In 1903 a large stove was moved into the main room with the proviso that no child should sit within four or five feet of it. The head teacher had to ask for a guard for it. The stove seemed to work satisfactorily until 1925, when the caretaker broke the draught door. As the stove was filled, the fire began to burn furiously and considerable damage was done to the chest of drawers and the cupboard standing nearby.

By 1906 the inspector was congratulating the managers on the improvement they had effected. This was in marked contrast to the report he had given the previous year, which read:

> The playground and the base walls of the school are very damp. The offices should be regularly supplied with requisites and one of them should be adapted for the use of infants. The door in the dividing fence was open and the fence itself broken. The cloak room accommodation for the older children is decidedly inadequate. A better lavatory should also be provided. Many seats are rough, too narrow and often too far from the desks. The cleaning is not well done.

Although many of the suggestions were acted upon, the inspector noted in 1907 that the door of one of the closets needed repair. In 1908 he said that the lavatories (wash basins) should be provided with nail brushes and pumice stones. It should be noted that there was no running water at this stage. The inspector again wrote that the seats in the offices were all too high for the infants and the fences needed repair.

During this time the church was being restored and according to the parish marriage register the school room was licensed for weddings.

For the next few years no comments were made in the school log books about the buildings until in 1920 the head teacher noted that Mrs. Dockar-Drysdale had sent curtains to divide the classes in the upper school. In September 1922 workmen were occupying the building, which resulted in it being closed for an extra week's holiday.

The Board of Managers received a very comprehensive report of the state of the school in August 1924 and it read as follows:

> Report on the premises of the Radley C. of E. School made by HMI
> Mr. A. F. Page on the occasion of his visit to the school on 9th July 1924.

1. The school premises are picturesque and on the whole satisfactory for the numbers in attendance which average about 40. The defects in the premises would however be greatly accentuated if the number were increased to the figure (86), which represents the official accommodation.

2. Lighting in the classroom is satisfactory but is not very good in the main room. This room contains only a small skylight and some rather low built windows in front of the children. The lighting is not improved by a heavy curtain which when used shuts off a good deal of the light from one of the classes.

3. The school generally has an untidy look owing to the number of boxes and other articles lying about and the use of the fireplaces for waste paper. It is an important part of the training of the children that they should be taught in clean and tidy premises. The untidiness is increased by a bird's nest containing young birds in one of the beams in the main room.

4. A number of dilapidations need attention. Thus, the doors of some of the offices are off their hinges and the paint on the outside of the school should be renewed otherwise the woodwork will deteriorate.

5. There does not appear to be any supply of water for either the school house or the school.

I am to request that the HMI's report may receive attention and that the Board may be informed what steps it is proposed to take in regard to a water supply for the school.

The offices, or toilets as we now call them, consisted of pails under planks of wood with suitable holes cut in them. The pails were supposed to be emptied at least three times per week by the caretaker. In October 1915 there was a directive from the Education Secretary for Berkshire, Mr. M. F. Anderson, to the Rev. Longland suggesting that the pails should be emptied on to the school teacher's garden. He said that for a small school only a small space was needed and that 2 to 3 poles in measurement would be sufficient, but the garden would need turning over each time. He said it would be better to empty the pails frequently and that once a day was best. He continued that no complaint had been received from other schools when this was done and in suitable soil the same ground could be used after about a fortnight. He added that all offices and cloakrooms should contain a box with dry earth in them. In April 1917 new pails were bought at a cost of £1 . 7 . 0 but this meant that the back of the offices had to be altered to take them costing a further £1 . 3 . 6. It is possible that the caretaker did not always take the contents of the pails very far as the following report appeared in the log book of November 1924:

I received a letter this morning from the Education Secretary telling me the school should remain closed until the heap in the school yard was cleared. The scholars were sent home and the heap cleared away in the afternoon.

A year after the inspector had noted that there was no water supply to the school, the Berkshire Education Committee Secretary visited the school regarding its installation. It seems to have been provided because by the end of 1927 there was a problem with blocked sinks in the lobby.

In 1928 another window was added on the north side, but the wall was showing signs of giving way. Another iron girder had to be attached to the building to support it.

For the first time, offices for the boys are mentioned in 1931, as workmen had to repair the woodwork around them and also the roof. At the same time the workmen filled in the well, which until mains water arrived was the likely source of water for the school and school house. The filling in of the well must not have been carried out very thoroughly as it caved in after a coal cart carrying a ton of coal went over it in 1937. A hole 1½ ft. by 2½ ft. by 1½ ft. deep appeared. It gave way again in 1939.

The head teacher, Mrs. Agnes F. M. Smith (née Pendleton), gained permission from the vicar, the Rev. Arthur Aubert Jackson, in 1932, to have the front of the school house ground altered, at her expense. The existing hedge was cut down and a path made directly to the back gate of the vicarage. A new hedge was planted around the ground making the house more private. This meant that the girls could walk along a path to their offices and had a definite area for their playground. (Boys and girls still had separate playgrounds). In 1936 a shed was built at the side of the boys' playground for bicycles.

In October 1932 the children were excused lessons for 10 minutes while a man came to gas the mice holes in the school.

The caretaker was ill for a short time at the beginning of 1933. A local lady was called in to help with the fires but the teachers had difficulty keeping the stove alight. For a while all the children had to work in the infant classroom as it was warmer. The children helped with the preparation of the classroom, but there was no one to attend to the offices.

Before November 1933 the walls around the infant classroom had caused concern so workmen in that month were called in to repair them. The men dug to the foundations and placed cement under the walls. After they had finished the school yard became unusable as a large amount of gravel had been left behind. The boys used a wire rake to smooth over the ground and collect as many stones as possible. Another hazard discovered during this time was the loose, barbed-wire fencing at the edge of the farmer's field. It had to be replaced when one child cut her leg badly on it. The head teacher borrowed iodine from a neighbour and applied it well after washing the leg with boiling water. (Hopefully it was cooled before use!) The child was able to return to school in the afternoon but her mother went up to the school in the evening to see the vicar, the Rev. Arthur Jackson, and Mr. Greening, the farmer.

At the beginning of 1935 the flooring gave way in the school room and had to be repaired.

The head teacher had quite a shock on the morning of March 30th 1936 when she found the school on fire. Fire brigades from Abingdon and Radley College were in attendance. No mention was made in the school log books as to the cause of the fire but it caused a fair amount of damage. Pictures, a piano and one wall cupboard full of books were burnt. A chair was spoiled. Dusters, towels and cleaning apparatus were destroyed along with hoops, skipping ropes and 30 pairs of gym shoes. The school was closed for about three weeks, which included the Easter holidays, as windows and doors had to be repaired and the school and its contents cleaned. A short while afterwards Mr. Slade (probably an official from Berkshire Education Committee) and a fire insurance officer examined the damaged stock.

Throughout 1938 and 1939 there were times when the yard flooded, causing problems when the children wanted to go to the offices. Keys had been supplied for the offices because of 'information received during the vacation'. Pails were still being used as the caretaker was reprimanded for not scraping them well enough. Many people would have sympathy with him. A new water supply, however, was going to be installed in October 1939.

Problems with the yard continued into 1940. It often flooded and only children with wellingtons could get into their porch. There was a large quantity of bricks left around from the alterations to the chimneys and the boys were given the task of filling the large holes in the playground with them.

The ceiling in the infants' room again fell down in 1941. It was repaired at the same time as the school roof. Protective wire was fixed to the skylight.

During the war Radley School was earmarked as a suitable reception centre for Oxford citizens in case the city should receive a severe bombing. Miss Cross, the head teacher by then, agreed that blankets and food could be stored in the school provided they were in a box or chest. She informed the officials who were dealing with the situation that the school key was kept in her house but should she be away they had better break in the lock of the infants' door. In March 1941 the equipment for the rest centre arrived and caused more congestion for storage space. This was even more noticeable when further stock was delivered in May and again in August. A hanging cupboard and 40 chairs for the rest centre were sent. Eventually Mr. Greening agreed to store the equipment at the farm. It was decided that the cycle shed could be used for extra offices and the Public Assistance Department would supply hessian and Elsan closets in the event of a blitz on Oxford. The school was given two sand bags which, together with the three they had made, meant they had a grand total of five for the school and house. The rest centre requisites were removed in February 1945.

The population of the school had grown considerably by 1942 but the managers were informed that it was impossible to build any new buildings during the war. The fabric of the buildings was deteriorating too and this wasn't helped when a gale in February 1943 caused several tiles to come off the roof. The hanging tiles on the school house were loose and one fell off, narrowly missing a child. The back door of the school to the playground broke in 1944, making it impossible to lock. The managers were informed that it was not possible to grant a permit for wood to repair the door so the school had to remain unlocked.

At the beginning of 1945, the chief electrician of the Wessex Electricity Company called at the school to discuss the possibility of electric light being installed providing the necessary permit was forthcoming. In April of that year the workmen installed the light fittings and they were connected to the main later in the month.

The first months of 1947 were notorious for being severely cold and the classrooms could not be kept warm. By this time, the large numbers of children in school meant that the parish room at the vicarage was being used. In the extremely cold weather all the children and staff went in there as it was easier to keep this room warm. The playground was still in a dreadful state, as the soakaways were blocked and overflowing. To cap it all there was a ban on the use of electricity, which resulted in the new lighting system not being used, and the shortage of coke prevented the stoves from being used. There was a small amount of coal but this could only be burnt in the small grate in the large room. The plaster on the ceiling above that grate and its surrounds was dangerous, which meant that the children could not sit near to it. The plaster eventually fell down a few months later and the whole ceiling had to be removed as it was not safe. The caretaker was absent during these hard times and his work was done by local ladies at the going rate of 2 shillings per hour. The whole picture in the later war years, and for the few years following, seemed to be very gloomy.

Good news came in September 1949 when a new building was begun. This was to be a canteen but, because of the workmen and their digging of a trench to take water to the new building, the playground was again in an awful state. The only piece the children could use was the path to the gate. In November of that year the playground was under 6 inches of water. It was impossible to get to the offices or to the infant classroom by going outside. Miss Cross described the playground in February 1950 as being like 'thick cream with mud'. Prior to the canteen being built, the County Architect, Mr. H. J. Knowles, sent a plan to the Rev. Pixell of an Orlit hut which had been erected at Speenhamland Primary School, near Newbury. Orlit huts consisted of iron stanchions 8 feet apart with walls made of concrete blocks fashioned from crushed, cemented, blast furnace waste. It was a pre-fabricated building with a flat roof. The building known as the canteen at Radley School looks very like this.

In February 1950 the canteen was finished but because of the overcrowding in the school the dining room part of it had to be used for an infant class. Later two classes were using it.

The canteen.

There were changes too in the sanitary arrangements when a cesspool, under the area now used as a staff car-park, was connected to Radley College drainage system.

Relief for the playground came at last in March 1950 when workmen arrived to put a tar surface on it. The boys removed the good soil from the old gardens beforehand.

Dimensions for the school, given about this time, were:

	Classroom 1	Classroom 2	Canteen
Length	29' 6"	19' 6"	29' 6"
Breadth	17' 6"	16' 6"	23' 6"
Height	11½ '	12½ '	

It was not long before the canteen building had problems. The tank had to be removed and alterations made to the kitchen because of bad condensation. By January 1952 the ceiling of the kitchen was falling in and had to be repaired.

24

The people of Radley were aware of the need for a new school and in the *Radley Parish Magazine* of September 1951 the vicar, the Rev. John Vincent Pixell, was writing that there had been a fete at Radley College in aid of the new village school fund. Just over £120 was raised and there would have been more if he hadn't had to pay the college £1 . 6 . 3 for missing cups and saucers. In the same magazine he wrote about this and said, 'It would seem that people today have little idea of ownership, and take anything they see if they happen to want it'.

The school became a controlled school in 1951 under the provisions of the Education Act 1944. According to the vicar, writing in the *Parish Magazine* in November 1951, the parish would have had to have raised a large amount of money to keep it as an aided school. He hoped a fairy godmother or an Aladdin's lamp would come along and find the £13,000 required but it was unlikely in a village with few big houses and mainly working people. In May 1952 the vicar wrote that in order to save the school as an aided school the managers would have to guarantee £288 . 10 . 0 per annum for 50 years, which they felt was an impossibility. Subscribers to the fund for building a new school were asked whether their donations, totalling over £655, should be given to the diocese for other church schools or be used in the parish at the discretion of the church managers. This was because the County Council became responsible for the building of new premises rather than the church. No mention was made of where the money went to.

In May 1954 Mr. David J. Buckle, as representative of the Parish Council and a school manager, produced a report on the state of the school. With his kind permission the following shows some of what he found:

Exterior

a. Sanitary Arrangements. These are very bad indeed. There are only six buckets, three for boys and three for girls. Although they are emptied daily it would be an improvement if Elsan pans could replace them.

b. The condition of the building, which stands in its own ground, is very bad and appears to be very draughty.

c. The roof is of tiles and, when standing inside, light can be seen through in many places where rain must come in during heavy showers.

d. Playground. This is very small for the number of children attending the school and has a bad surface. There are no playing fields for such games as football, etc. A path leads from the playground to the main road but there is no safety barrier to prevent children running straight into the road.

e. Duck pond. There is a pond 25 yards from the playground which during the greater part of the year is covered in green slime and gives a foul smell. This pond was cleaned out in 1953 but is as bad as ever.

f. Accommodation. There are 112 children at a school which was built for 80 with the possibility of an increase in numbers on roll. The two main classrooms are not overcrowded but a dining room which was built to hold one class is now holding two infant classes and is BADLY overcrowded.

g. Washing facilities. There are only six bowls which are situated in an outhouse and there is only one cold tap. Hot water is brought from the kitchen. The outhouse is very small and used for the children's outdoor clothing.

h. Heating. Classrooms are heated by three stoves, two burning coke and one anthracite. The stoves are very dusty, take up a lot of room and do not have adequate guards around them.

i. Ceiling. There is a high gable ceiling which must take away a lot of heat from the classroom. An artificial ceiling has been erected in one part of the main class room and could be extended to cover the other.

j. Floors. Made of wood planks and in a very bad condition.

k. Interior decoration. The walls and paint work are in a bad condition and need painting. They have not been painted since the war.

Mr. Buckle went on to recommend that a new classroom should be built and a building erected to hold proper sanitary arrangements with space for wash basins and sufficient hanging space for the children's outdoor clothes. He suggested that the playground should be expanded and the interior of the building be redecorated. These recommendations were eventually acted upon but the school had to be patient for a few more months.

New windows were put into the school building in 1954 and the main building redecorated. Because of the large enrolment, for some days each week the village hall, located just over the railway bridge in Lower Radley, had to be used for classes. In the *Parish Magazine*, Miss Cross thanked Mr. and Mrs. E. Turner of Stonhouse Crescent, Radley, for the gift of a push chair to convey books, etc., backwards and forwards to the hall. As the hall is over half a mile from the school this must have proved very useful.

In 1955 the school was larger than it had ever been and there were 120 children on roll. A new wire mesh and concrete fence had been erected along the front of the school and later in the year a new timber floor was laid in the main building. The condition of the kitchen was appalling and HMI and Mr. Atkins were called in to see it. The roof needed tarring and this was done during the summer of 1955. In September, during the night, tar came through into the dining room where the infant class worked. To prevent any accidents happening to the children Classes I and II went home during the afternoons when the men were working. It wasn't a satisfactory job as the roof leaked over the kitchen in heavy rain later in the month.

The beginning of 1957 brought renewed hope to the school when builders started work on two new classrooms and a cloakroom block. The playground was once again a mud bath but everyone was very pleased when the new rooms became available after the summer holidays. The two younger classes moved into this building and the dining room became a hall and practical room. The playground was extended later in the year. Modern desks and chairs were supplied for the old building, which housed two classes separated by sliding doors. This area became very congested as there was no staffroom and virtually no storage space.

The dimensions of the school in September 1957 are as follows:

Old School

Large room 30' by 18' = 540 sq. ft.
Small room 20' by 17' = 340 sq. ft.
Large Cloakroom 7' 6" by 10' 6" = 79 sq. ft. approx.
Small Cloakroom 8' by 6' = 48 sq. ft. approx.   Total = 1007 sq. ft

In pencil
Cloakroom 7' by 6' = 42 sq. ft.
11' by 7.75' = 85.25 sq. ft.

Canteen

Dining room (Crossed out in the relevant log book).
30' by 24' = 720 sq. ft. app.

New building

Classrooms. 23' 3" by 21' 9" = 2(505) sq. ft.
Each with alcoves 9' by 3' = 2(27)sq. ft.
Cloak room area.
23' by 11' = 253 sq. ft.
Passage area 11' by 5' = 55 sq. ft.

2 x Lavatory accommodation

13' by 11' = 2 (143) sq. ft.
Boys = 3 WCs + 1 urinal + 5 wash basins + 1 drinking fountain.
Girls = 5 WCs and 5 wash basins + 1 drinking fountain.
Total 1638 sq. ft.

Total area for daily cleaning = 1007 sq. ft. + 720 sq. ft. + 1638 sq. ft.
= 3365 sq. ft.

In 1958 some of the brickwork of the old building was showing its age and woodwork in the porches was disintegrating. The big porch, riddled with woodworm and with rotten lower boards, was completely stripped in 1959, lined with hardboard and painted. The sink was removed to the large classroom and the entrance door was replaced as it was considered to be in a very poor condition. The paved playground was not big enough for organised activities, but it was resurfaced. At this stage there was no field available. Two years later the playground was extended beyond the canteen and the playing field was levelled and grassed.

With pupil numbers remaining high and more accommodation needed there was great excitement at the school when information arrived to say that a new building would be in the 1963 County Council schedule. This would consist of a hall, classroom, staff room, head teacher's room, library space and entrance space.

Memories of 1947 came back to many people in 1963 when there was another severe winter. The head teacher, Miss Cross, was worried that, on one occasion, the school was down to one day's supply of coke. Many pipes were frozen and she recorded a temperature of minus 32 deg F. on January 25th. She remarked that the River Thames had frozen over.

After the 1963 summer holidays Kimberleys of Oxford had almost completed the new buildings but there were problems with the oil-fired heating system. Eventually in November the staff were able to use the staff room and, towards the end of December, Miss Middleton's class of infants moved into their new room using their existing furniture as the new allocation had not arrived. The next day the school used the hall for prayers. There seemed to be a problem with the acoustics of the building as a whole and complaints were sent to Berkshire County Council's Director of Education and the architect. The following appeared in the log book about this time:

<u>Measurements of the new building in December 1963 in square feet</u>

Staff room - 131
Staff cloakroom - 47
Hall - 1221.25
Classroom - 520.5 and 138.25
Entrance hall and cloakroom - 270
Cloakroom passage - 23.5
Library space - 231.25
Head Teacher's room - 133.5
Passage - 35.25
Total area = 2751.25

Measurements of old canteen in November 1969 - 42' by 24' = 1008 sq. ft.
Measurements of kitchen in November 1969 - approx. 40' by 22' = 929 sq. ft.
less 18' by 5' = 90 sq. ft.
Total area = 839 sq. ft.

Total area for cleaning = 6287.25
Total area of kitchen = 839.

The kitchen staff had worked valiantly in the cramped conditions they had and were pleased when, in 1966, the kitchen was enlarged by taking some space off the dining room. The school managers and the Parish Council were aware of the cramped conditions for the children in the school and in November 1966 they started a campaign for an extra classroom. There was an article in the *Oxford Mail* reporting the fact that representatives of the council and managers would be meeting Mr. Richard West, chairman of the Berkshire Planning Committee, to discuss the problem. Mr. David Buckle, chairman of the Parish Council, said that the strongest possible representations must be made to the County Council and the Education Committee. He said that the school was built for 120 children and it already had 141 with another 20 expected at the beginning of the next term and the summer term. He also said that the situation was serious as there was a great lack of proper space for the children and there was a dire necessity for a new classroom. Radley was expanding fast and it was obvious that there would be more growth and development which would put even more pressure onto the already inadequate school buildings. One of the main problems at the school was that the assembly hall/gymnasium had to be used as a classroom. Mr. Buckle said that the acoustics in the hall were the worst in the country. The chairman of the school managers, Mr. J. Gowring, agreed that there should be no delay in pressurising the County. The Director of Education replied that applications for classrooms were considered by the Committee according to the need of the school and the financial situation and these were kept under review. He admitted some schools were better off than Radley but others were in a worse condition.

In 1967 the playground was drained ready for tarring and the old bicycle shed was torn down and a new one erected behind the old lavatories, after the coal bunkers had been removed.

Pleas for more accommodation fell on deaf ears at Berkshire County Council as money was in short supply, but the committee agreed that a new kitchen could be built at the end of the hall and the canteen could be converted into a classroom. This was begun in 1969. It was not without its difficulties and frustrations. On one occasion Miss Cross upset the workmen when she insisted that the gates were locked. This was the only way she would know when lorries would be going over the playground otherwise it would be a danger to the children who were having to play at the front of the school as the workmen had taken over the remainder of the playground area. On another occasion, when the workmen wanted to break through into the hall, everything had to be moved out of there. The workmen agreed to make some ramps in order that the piano, etc. could be moved out but the foreman refused to let them do it as making ramps was not in his contract. Miss Cross informed him that she would not move out of the hall until ramps had been made by an outside firm. The foreman relented and ramps were made that day. The workmen were again out of favour when they spread gravel over the playground and the caretaker threatened to resign unless the workmen kept off the floor he had cleaned after the painters had finished. On completion of the alterations it was discovered that there was no mesh over the kitchen window. The architect decided to put one on with a depth of 6 inches, which caused a hazard to children going past it. The Director of Education received a complaint from Miss Cross.

The new kitchen finally came into use in October 1969. Mr. Osborne, one of the teachers, had to use the hall as a classroom while half of it was used as a dining room. The builders then knocked down the wall in the canteen and renovated the room ready for when it became a classroom. Unfortunately it could not be used at first because the architect had failed to make provision in the plans for any form of heat. It took a while for the architect and the Local Education Authority to decide whose responsibility it was but eventually, in January 1970, Mr. Osborne was able to move into the old canteen.

In May 1970 the managers recommended that the field be drained and that the two toilets, removed from the boys' cloakroom, should be replaced. They also wanted a toilet fitted in the old building as it was felt that children should not be expected to have to go across 50 yards of playground to use it. More importantly there was a danger from vans, etc. crossing the playground to visit the kitchen. In autumn 1970 the old building was retiled and a false ceiling fitted. A new floor had to be laid in the kitchen as the tiles were too far apart.

When Mr. Stephens became head teacher in 1974, he and Mr. Lee, one of the teachers, spent a lot of time after school improving the classrooms in the old building. The builders replaced the wainscotting and the two teachers installed wall-mounted work benches. The library area was improved with carpeting and pin boards were covered with hessian. The Education Committee encouraged head teachers to go on a course in Oxford to learn how to do small repairs in schools and Mr. Stephens attended it.

In 1976 a parent complained about the boys' toilets. There was only one urinal for 70 + boys and it obviously needed replacing. This was done later in the year, with a much more sanitary arrangement. Mr. Stephens had been complaining for some time but the complaint from a parent speeded it up.

During December 1977 gas central heating was installed and at the beginning of 1978 thoughts were given to roof insulation as parts of the school were very cold in winter. This was done in 1980.

Parents gradually played a greater part in the life of the school as time went by and in December 1980 a group of parents built a stage for the school hall.

Repairs continued to be done during the next few years. The staff room was refurbished, painting of the exterior was carried out, rotten timber was replaced, the canteen was painted as the paint was flaking off the walls and curtains were made for the hall and old building.

In 1987 a new heating system was installed.

On March 1st 1990 a roofing contractor asked for a 999 call as he had discovered a fire in the roof space where he had been felting. The fire brigade attended but by then the fire was out. The children were not evacuated from the building but were prepared to be, if necessary. In August of that year parents decorated Bowyer classroom.

During 1993 the old building, at that time called Stonhouse, had a concrete floor laid. New windows were installed on the south side of the main building and safety film was put on all windows. The following year, during the summer holidays, the school was partly redecorated and a new pitched roof was put over two classrooms.

For the years 1994 to 1995 plans were made to renew the remaining hall windows, decorate the exterior of the school and replace the facilities in the junior toilets. It was hoped to completely renew all windows, renew lead water mains and sky lights and to have Thames classroom's roof renewed.

In 1998, helped by the College boys, a gravel path was laid from the car park to the school. The gravel was donated by Tuckwells.

The school underwent some positive refurbishment in 2000. The main foyer area was carpeted and peg stands were removed to provide additional teaching space. The kitchen area had some new cupboards and tiles. The library was equipped with more books, using money from donations given in memory of the late Joy Alexander, who had been closely connected with the school as a governor for many years.

The newly formed pre-school had a fully functional outdoor play area in 2000 with a safe play surface, a large sandpit and covered deck area.

As numbers increased in 2001 there was need for an extra classroom. The old kitchen, redundant since school dinners were no longer cooked on the premises, was transformed into a room for the reception class. The fund-raising committee raised £11,000 in 6 months, nearly half the cost of the conversion. The inspectors had recommended this new classroom as, previously, there had been a mixed reception and infants' class. The final target of

£22,000 was reached just before Christmas 2001. A little before then, it was discovered that extra money was needed due to a change in the heating requirements. With a forward loan from the LEA the extra money was found and the project went ahead. Fund raising had to continue for some time afterwards. Many local organizations gave donations towards the new Windrush classroom. It was formally opened on Friday, February 22nd 2002 by Danny Sullivan, the Director of Education for the diocese. As a result of the new classroom the school in 2002 had four rooms for its 75 children. The old building was no longer used for classrooms and for a while it was used by the after-school club 'Rascals'.

Early in 2007 the Governors were pleased to announce that £400,000 had been raised, through various grants, to go ahead with the building of a new classroom for the Joint Foundation Unit. The head teacher and her staff will also have meeting rooms, where they can enjoy better facilities.

At the time of writing this book, the school awaits the completion of this new classroom to replace the old canteen, which will be pulled down. The old building is to have a new damp-proof course fitted and repairs carried out to the roof.

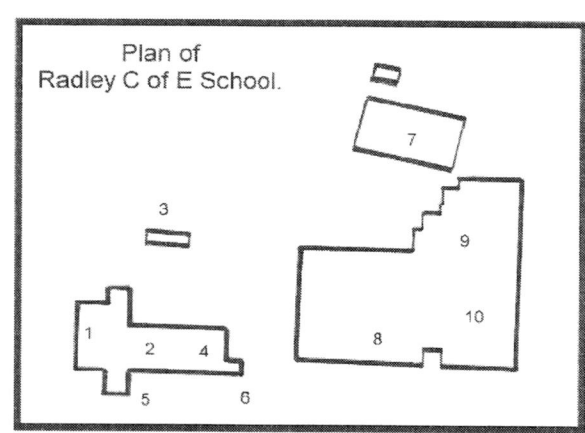

Key
1.   School house.
2.   1873 school building.
3.   Offices (toilets)built in 1891.
4.   Infant classroom added 1892.
5.   Lavatory added 1895.
6.   Cloakroom added 1905.
7.   Canteen built in 1950.
8.   Two new classrooms, toilet and cloakroom block 1957.
9.   Kitchen built in 1969.
10.   Hall, staff room, head teacher's room, classroom, library space, entrance hall and cloakrooms built in 1963.

Chapter 2

The People 1851 - 1876

Head Teachers

John Palmer - About 1851 - ?
John Robinson - 1859 - ?
Thomas Emerton - About 1861 - ?
Mr. Bower - About 1866 to December 1867.
? - January 1868 - December 1868.
H. S. Clarke - December 1868 - November 1870.
B. Basson - (1 week only).
Harriet Hardiman - November 1870 - July 1872.
Miss Miller - December 1872.
Sarah Anne Jones - January 1873 - January 1874.
Miss M Walters - March 1874 - June 1875.
Miss G. E. Pearson -July 1875 - August 1875.
H. M. Walker - September 1875 - December 1875.
C. Turner - January 1876 - April 1876.

Assistant Teachers

Mrs. Turner - About 1870.
Harriet Robinson - November 1870 - July 1872.
Miss Sims - About January 1873 - April 1874.

Monitress

Kate Prior - About 1875

There are no records currently available to inform us who the village school masters or mistresses were before Radley School's log books commenced and the censuses giving details of occupations began. The log books sometimes omitted the name of the writer, which causes difficulties in knowing, between the censuses, who the head teachers were.

According to the census of 1851 John Palmer was the Radley village school master. John, who lived from about 1791 to 1857, had married Harriet Dean from Southmoor in 1831 and they had 14 children. At least four died in infancy but many of the others lived to adulthood. Harriet also worked as a laundress. It is not known who followed him as school master, but it is known that in 1859 it was John Robinson. He left before 1861, for in that year he and his wife Sarah and their two children were living in Northamptonshire.

In 1861 Thomas Emerton was in charge of Radley School. He had previously been a teacher in Yorkshire and after living in Radley he went to Staffordshire, the county where he and his wife, a school mistress, were born. He left Radley at some time before 1867.

The school log books commenced in 1866, possibly when Mr. Bower became the headmaster, and from this point onwards many more records are available. School attendance was not compulsory at this time and the picture painted by the early entries in the first log book is of a frustrated teacher who had problems with the punctuality and attendance of his pupils. The school building was in a very poor condition and the school was over half a mile away from the majority of the population. At many times during the agricultural year the children were of far more use to their parents at home rather than at school.

The first known HMI report for Radley School was in 1866, when the inspector commented on the fact that the school was conducted by a young school master who seemed to be interested in his work. The next report in November 1867, when Mr. Bower was mentioned as the teacher, was not a favourable one. The inspector wrote that the needlework was not systematically taught, the reading was taught unskilfully, the dictation was moderate, the arithmetic fair, copy books pretty fair and the intelligence of the children should be cultivated more. As a result of the unfavourable report the school was informed that, unless improvements were made in the teaching, the grant made by the Privy Council Office would be reduced the following year and Mr. Bower would not be receiving his certificate. Seventeen children had been examined and 75% had passed. Mr. Bower finished at the school the following month.

Berkshire Record Office, in Reading, has copies of entries in the Radley School cash account book for 1867 to 1888 and these give an interesting insight into the financial situation of the school at that time. The following is a selection from the entries for the years 1867 to 1870:

<u>November 1st 1867 - October 1868</u>

Receipts
Privy Council Grant	£16 . 3 . 4
School pence	£6 . 17 . 1
Parish Vestry	£10
Offertory St. Peter's College	£10

Payments.

Master's salary	£50
Sewing Mistress	£4
Pemberton for coals	10s . 6d
Fisher for firewood	2s . 6d
National Society for 3 new desks	£6 . 11 . 9
Payment for clock	16s
Shepherd for coal box	2s . 3d
Cleaning	5s
Sir Geo. Bowyer's rent	£1 . 6 . 0

1868 - 1869

Receipts.

Privy Council Grant	£13 . 10 . 11
St. Peter's College	£10
School pence	£ 5 . 6 . 1
Subscription from E.E. Morris Esq.	£ 1

Payments.

Master's salary	£50
Sewing Mistress	£ 3
Rent of School	£ 1 . 6 . 0

1869 - 1870

Receipts

Privy Council Grant February	£ 9 . 18 . 3
Privy Council Grant August	£ 5 . 2 . 2

Payments.

H. H. Clarke's salary	£18
Sewing Mistress	£ 1 . 2 . 6
B. Basson (only remained one week)	11s . 6d
H. Hardiman	£ 3 . 3 . 3

On January 16th 1868, the first day for the new head teacher, whose name wasn't given, the attendance was only 8 out of 49 on roll. This was because the first day of the school week was a Thursday and the parents felt they were not getting their money's worth for only two days' education in that week. It was often a problem collecting money for the school fees from parents and there was much irregularity over payments. Families were often very large and this payment was a drain on their meagre resources.

Attendance and punctuality continued to be a problem and featured prominently in the first log book. On April 30th 1868 the Westons and the Comleys stayed away on account of 'garlanding' (making garlands for May Day). In July many children were absent on account of 'field work'. In August of that year school could not begin on the appointed day because of Radley Feast. A week later school began in earnest but some children were still absent as they were 'fagging', i.e., helping to gather barley. Many children stayed away for Hinksey Feast at the end of August. There was a ploughing match in Abingdon on 22nd September and a large number of parents allowed their children to miss school in order to watch. At the beginning of October the headmaster informed the children there would be no holiday for Abingdon Fair (sometimes called Abingdon Hiring Fair), but half the children went there anyway. Other reasons for not attending school included gleaning, gardening, bird minding, gathering acorns, going errands, baby minding, potato gathering, looking after sick family members, holidays, frightening crows (mainly by the girls), gathering peas, picking chestnuts and watching pigs and oxen. Attendance was often better when the weather was wet as the children could not work in the fields.

The age range of children at the school was from approximately 4 years to 13 years although not many children stayed at school until they were 13. Many children, especially boys, left school for work at an earlier age. In July 1868, James Hook left to go to work at the age of 11½. The school children were divided into Infants and Standards I to VII but all were taught in one room by one teacher, which caused many difficulties. It must have been an almost impossible task to keep the little children in order and occupied, when they were not capable of reading or writing, while the older children were being taught. The school had very limited resources in the classroom. Anne Silvester, a pupil, taught sewing for a while before Mrs. Welsh was able to help out, on a very part-time basis. On at least two occasions the headmaster appealed to the Warden at Radley College for a school mistress to assist him. In March 1868 the school started to employ Mrs. Turner, for mornings only, to help to look after the very little ones and this helped to keep the noise level down in the classroom. When the children started to be more regular in attendance, the head remarked that 'more energy was needed to secure order'. He began to feel that the behaviour of the children was getting better and they were cleaner.

In January 1868 the head teacher wrote that, when his back was turned, the very little ones were more noisy and mischievous than usual. One of the worst of these was the youngest of the Weston children who was between 4 and 5 years old. The head teacher scolded this 'pugnacious child' and used a little stick on him but it had no effect. Eventually the sister of the boy was asked by the headmaster not to bring him to school until he could behave himself. Corporal punishment was allowed and boys were caned for misbehaviour. The head even flogged some children for behaving inappropriately in church. Joseph Pocock was flogged and kept without his dinner for hitting girls. Charles Pocock was punished for taking an apple off the desk. The head teacher tried keeping in the youngest Weston and Minns after school one day in March and received an impertinent message from the parents as a result.

Harsh discipline was administered quite frequently for misbehaviour as the head teacher seemed to be having problems with discipline. In mid-1868 he wrote that the children were noisy, especially the younger ones, and that some were unruly and disorderly. He had to punish some of the little ones for plucking currants in the garden. Many of the boys were punished on a regular basis for bad behaviour and on one occasion they had to be warned for injuring Farmer Smith's trees. The parents of Eliza Grimes had to be called about her behaviour out of school.

The head teacher had other problems as well. There was no writing on paper one day as the ink was 'all clotted'. The ink jar later was knocked over and it cracked, causing some loss of ink. The Warden of Radley College had to caution children about ink covers and the scratching of some new desks with their feet. The weather played a part in the teacher's difficulties and when there was a very heavy storm in July a fire had to be lit to dry pinafores.

Newspaper reading by the children was introduced and tables were practised while preparing for work at the opening of school. The head teacher noticed that, after a month, this had lapsed. He tried to introduce homework by sending home pieces of newspaper for home lessons on spelling and he later introduced a timetable because the second class were not regularly taught religious subjects. The school had a diocesan inspection each year and in 1868 the Rev. Clutterbuck, the diocesan inspector, strongly recommended drill. He also wrote that he objected to the obtrusive holding out of hands.

The headmaster at this time seems to have had a difficult time in the school and he wrote that he was very ill in November 1868. This probably caused his resignation and on December 8th 1868 Mr. H. S. Clarke became the headmaster.

Mr. Clarke found the school in a poor state and wrote:

> The children are very undisciplined. At first I attributed their ill behaviour to the arrogance which is always taken by children at the change of master. But I find that they must be treated with the greatest strictness to ensure anything like orderly conduct. The behaviour of children in church is very bad. Some of the bigger boys who only attend the Sunday school and over whom the master has no control set a shockingly bad example to the younger ones.

The inspector reported, shortly after Mr. Clarke had started at the school, that parallel desks had been introduced but the school-keeping was deficient in skill and firmness. He felt that the methods of teaching were capable of considerable improvement, that mental arithmetic should be introduced and the children's intelligence should be more fully developed. The inspector reduced the grant by one tenth and hoped to see an improvement in the following year. Unfortunately there was none and the grant was then reduced by two tenths.

Mr. Clarke seemed to take the criticism on board and commenced a plan to give marks to children for their work as an incentive to be more industrious. They were given extra help with dictation as he found them to be very poor at it. He made the 1st and 2nd classes (the older children) write from memory as much of the scripture lesson given the day before as they could recollect. There were some curious specimens of composition produced. He noted that he had taught long multiplication and short division to the 2nd class and then he wrote that they were stupid about arithmetic a couple of weeks later. A month later he was teaching compound rates. This was quickly followed by the comment that the 2nd class were very dull with their arithmetic but they were learning money tables. In June 1869 he wrote that the younger children in the 4th class were very backward and he thought it would remain like this until the school had an alphabet card. He received the card and a box of chalk during the following week. The first and second classes were each given sponges as they had developed the disgusting habit of licking their slates.

On the 2nd July the boys swept the room for the first time since May 1st, but the broom was worn out and a new one was requested.

The poor ability of the children was not surprising considering the amount of absenteeism and the lateness of the children at the commencement of school. In December 1868, soon after Mr. Clarke had taken charge, several boys were late one morning. They had stayed to see a pig killed at W. Smith's. The head caned them and kept them in double the time they were late. Truancy was a problem. James and William Hook and W. Silvester were suspected of playing truant on several occasions. Children were also absent from school through illness. Charles Comley had scarlet fever in February 1869. His sister Emily was sent home as it was not safe to have any children from their house at the school.

The headmaster had reason to be absent himself on 12th March 1869 as he had to appear at the Assize held in Aylesbury on an 'unfounded charge made against him'. Shortly afterwards the Rev. Clutterbuck, the diocesan inspector, wrote that:

> The discipline and general tone of the school were much improved. The reading
> showed that pains had been taken in teaching distinct utterance.

There were 39 on roll at this time made up of 20 boys and 19 girls. The school was also having less trouble collecting the fees, but there were still times when children had to be sent home to collect their pennies.

Nuneham Fete was a popular attraction on July 6th 1869. All the pupils, except for Thomas Young who arrived at school on that day, were absent in order to attend the fete. The children were allowed a holiday on 27th July as the Radley village cricket club were playing Radley College servants' club. Another half-day's holiday was given when the village team played Littlemore, the time being made up at the beginning or end of the main holidays. Summer holidays for the school children were never determined until it was known when the harvest was ready to be brought in and this could vary considerably. If the harvest hadn't been brought in completely by the time the school holiday finished, there would be many children absent. On October 11th the head wrote, 'Many children are still employed in field work and several of the best have been regularly unpayed (sic) by the farmers'.

It was not surprising that when the Rev. Wood visited the school to examine various standards the children were not very successful. The head teacher wrote that his pupils were unaccustomed to having a visitor in school and the attendance record of most of the children was very poor, their having been engaged in potato picking and other field work.

As a result of the poor government examination in October 1869, the headmaster decided to start to teach English grammar, which would enable the school to receive an extra grant in the following year. He tried to explain the poor report by the fact that the school only knew about ten days prior to the inspection that it would take place and he had not been able to 'work the children up' in the subjects. His other excuse was that the reading books had only been in the school for a short time before the examination and they were quite new and strange to the children who had to read from them.

Only 13 children were present on March 1st 1870 as it was Shrove Tuesday and the children had gone around the village begging or, as the children termed it, 'Shroving'.

In the log book entry for 4th April 1870 Mr. Clarke wrote that he had admitted Mary Sadler, aged four years three months. He added, 'She is only a cause of disorder in the class and occupies all her sister's time instead of allowing her to pay attention to her work'. Mary was the youngest of 14 children of Jacob and Elizabeth Sadler, six of whom died in infancy or childhood. Of Isaac Villebois, who was about the same age as Mary when he started school, the headmaster wrote, 'He is much too young to get any good at school'. The average attendance at the school about this time was 35.

In May the Rev. Barber visited the school to present Frank East with a prayer book, the prize of the diocesan inspector. Edward Barber was the curate at Radley Church from about 1869 to 1883, during the whole of the incumbency of Charles Martin and part of the incumbency of Robert James Wilson, who were both in turn Wardens of Radley College. The Rev. Barber lived in Radley vicarage and his sons Edward, Arthur William and Cyril Frederick were all baptised at Radley in 1870, 1873 and 1876 respectively.

June 1870 brought another unsatisfactory report from the inspector. The condition of the school was imperfect, which meant that there was another reduction of the grant. Also the issue of the teacher's certificate was suspended until greater improvement was shown. Mr. Clarke remained at the school until November 3rd of that year, then left.

It seems as if a new broom really swept in when Harriet Hardiman arrived as the new head mistress. One of the first activities she initiated, which was not very popular, was to ask the boys to sweep the school clean in turn with the girls. She often sent children home to wash themselves, once with one boy going home and not returning. She introduced a system of teaching called Miss Miller's system. Miss Miller was probably the lady who was the principal of a training college at 104 St. Aldate's in Oxford at the time of the 1871 census. This could also have been the person who was paid a salary for the month of December when the school was rebuilt in 1872. Miss Miller, who was born in about 1825 in Walkeringham, Nottinghamshire, was described as an 'Educationalist (school mistress)' on the 1881 census and by that time she had moved to Wokingham in Berkshire. Harriet Anna Hardiman was born in Islington in 1848, the daughter of Thomas Hardiman, a labourer. According to the 1871 census, Harriet had the assistant mistress Harriet Robinson, aged 20, residing with her in the school house.

Miss Hardiman was keen to note in the log book that she was teaching scripture. The 1st class read *Kings of England* in December and *Ancient History* after Christmas.

Harriet Hardiman was not afraid to administer punishment and it is noted in the log books that she flogged five boys for being late, punished four boys for wilful disobedience and flogged William Silvester, Charles Pocock and Charles Comley for stealing Mr. George Silvester's rabbit traps. Charles Pocock's parents must have become used to his being sent home as on one occasion he used this as an excuse to stay there. Harriet wrote in the log book for April 24th that William Dawson had been playing truant and had spent his school money. She punished several children for running out of school at dinnertime in October. About the same time, John Pocock was punished for taking a pencil. He decided not to go back to school that afternoon.

Miss Hardiman was the head mistress of the school shortly after the Education Act of 1870 was introduced. This was known as Forster's Education Act after the MP of that name who drafted it. Its purpose was to provide elementary education for all children aged 5 to 10 years. At this time Parliament was aware of the need for Britain to remain competitive in the world, by being at the forefront in the manufacturing industries. There were also worries that Britain's status in world trade would be threatened by a lack of an effective education system. Some people were opposed to the Act, thinking that by educating the labouring classes they might start to think for themselves and realise they were leading dissatisfying lives and then revolt. Some churches opposed the Act as they feared losing their power to provide education for the poor. The Act allowed School Boards, elected by the rate payers, to provide primary education in areas where there was a need and also to pay the fees of poor children. Another part of the Act gave parents the right to withdraw their children from religious instruction, even in church schools. All schools would be inspected.

Miss Harriet Hardiman finished at the school in July 1872. It appears that this is the time that the new school was built and there are no entries in the log book until January 1873.

Sarah Jones became the new head teacher at the beginning of 1873 and her first entry in the log book said that it was the first day in the new building. The Rev. E. G. Barber visited the school on the first day to welcome her. Two weeks later he entertained the children for tea and in the evening he amused them with a magic-lantern show in the school room. The school then had 40 children on roll and had been supplied with new reading books and maps at the opening of the new building.

Towards the end of February the snow was very deep and the school had to be closed for a week.

A concession was made after the Easter holidays which enabled the children to attend for half price as it was only a three-day week. The children were given a day's holiday on May 1st in order that they could attend to their floral adornments and singing with which they usually welcomed this day.

An important day in the life of Radley was June 27th 1873, when the railway station opened. Many of the children absented themselves to watch the trains arrive.

The inspector's report of December 1873 was another unfavourable one. He said:

> The children were quite without interest in their studies. Writing is untaught and arithmetic is worthless. Reading is almost always quite imperfect and without intelligence. The little ones are restless and careless over their lessons.
>
> My Lords regret to receive so very unfavourable a report upon the general condition of the school. They have ordered the grant to be reduced by one tenth under Article 32/61 for defective instruction in arithmetic and they are unable to make any payment for the infants. Unless there is great improvement of the children next year, they may be compelled to withhold one half the grant.

Sarah Anne Jones resigned on January 27th 1874.

On March 2nd Miss M. Walters commenced her duties as mistress of the school. She made few comments in the log books until April 27th when she remarked that hooping (sic) cough and influenza colds were very prevalent in the village. Only 10 children had presented themselves at school and they were soon absent as they had colds. Attendances continued to be very low until June. Some days only four children were at school and the average attendance for the week ending May 23rd was 11.1.

There was another inspector's report in August 1874, which took into consideration the problem of the whooping cough outbreak. The inspector realised that little progress could be made at that time and he hoped that, by 'careful exercise of method and brisk discipline, the head would show at the next inspection well-founded and teachable classes'. As the present head teacher had made considerable improvements the school was given the full grant.

Miss Walters had problems with some girls but mainly with one called Elizabeth Beechey, who was aged about 10. On September 14th Elizabeth left the room but failed to return having taken Sarah Comley, aged about 8, with her. The following day Elizabeth arrived at the school at 9.40 a.m. and, on September 25th, with Caroline Woodley, she refused to cease singing when asked to do so. Also, while the head was out of the room to collect a child, Elizabeth Beechey rang the bell.

There is little information about punishments given by Miss Walters, but there are many entries about admissions and re-admissions. Pupil numbers fluctuated with children starting school and then stopping for such reasons as illness and family problems. For example, Annie Gibbens returned to school after a long absence on November 16th 1874 and Martha and Elizabeth Pocock could not attend school in December 1874 because they had chilblains. In February 1875 John Grimes returned to school after a long illness. Reuben and John Hook were not able to attend school for a while because of their shoes, presumably because they were not fit for winter weather.

The curriculum continued to expand with physical geography being introduced. Equipment seems to have been sparse as there are only a few occasions when it was recorded that the head mistress had received some new items. At the beginning of January she received 12 new slates, one set of arithmetical cards, a card to teach colour to infants, a card illustrating the first grades of form, some foolscap paper and a pointer. On March 25th she recorded:

> According to the requirements issued in the New Code of Regulation, I again commenced teaching grammar and geography. The Rev. Barber told me that as the rules would not be in force until August it was not required that I should do so at present.

Codes of Regulation for day schools were issued annually by the Government's Education Department from 1860 to 1900.

In April 1875 Daniel Weston, aged about 10, John Pocock, aged about 11, and William Carter left school to go to work.

On the 14th April some children were very late for the start of morning school and Miss Walters had to go some distance to meet them. Consequently it was 20 minutes to 10 before she could commence the scripture lesson. Lucy Woodley and Lucy Prior had gone out of their places, without permission, while she was away, which was against the school rules. When she sent them back to their places they kicked the school desk forms.

Miss Walters was no more successful than previous head teachers and was unable to survive the next inspection, which read:

> The work again this year seems to be an entire failure. Some children can read correctly enough to pass but their reading is almost always monotonous and unintelligent. Spelling and sums are quite imperfect and even the needlework and discipline are but moderate. My Lords cannot allow any grant for the infants in the face of the HMI report. One tenth has also been deducted from the grant to the elder children for faults of instruction. Miss Walters is leaving the school and for the present Miss G. E. Pearson will be in charge of it.

Miss Pearson stayed from the beginning of July until the summer or harvest holiday and earned £5. She was replaced in September by Mr. H. M. Walker, who undertook duties at the school until a certificated governess was found. He realised that the children were extremely backward. The first class was not able to do the simple rules and the reading and writing were 'bad'. He had the same problem of absenteeism as the other head teachers. There were no children in school one day in October, when it rained heavily. In December many children were absent because of snow.

In October Mr. Walker mentioned that he had made an error in the attendances because he had forgotten to subtract, from the summary, the attendances of Herbert Lay, born about 1873, who was under three years of age at that time. This meant that the age range of children in one class in one room was approximately 2 years to 13 years. It is difficult to imagine how anything was taught and how discipline could be maintained.

Miss C. Turner opened the school in January 1876 as its new head and found the children extremely backward in all subjects, with reading being especially poor. This head teacher felt the children showed no interest in their work and on several occasions she had to complain to them about the dirty state they were in when they came to school. The head teacher realised that reading and arithmetic lessons required immediate attention and dictation was a complete failure so needed to be commenced. Needlework was very disappointing and no intelligence was shown by the upper class. Starting in January, she gave dictation lessons to the first class. The children used slates and were given one or two words at a time. Spelling, the head found, was very faulty, especially the simple words. Miss Turner thought a good monitress was needed for the infants as they required more attention than could be given to them by her alone. By April the head noted that some progress was being made, especially in copy book writing, arithmetic, singing and in habits of cleanliness and punctuality. Miss Turner's salary for the time she was there amounted to £16 . 10 . 0. It was at this point that a new head teacher, Miss Julia Bell, took charge.

Radley Parish Church, which features prominently in the life of the village school.

Chapter 3

The People 1876 - 1892.

Head Teachers

Miss Julia Bell - 19th April1876 - 29th June 1882.
Miss Katherine Shaw - July 3rd 1882 - January 16th 1885.
Miss Mary J. Brewer - January 19th 1885 - December 30th 1888.
Miss Sarah A. Jarrett - January 7th 1889 - April 30th 1892.
Miss M. A. Charins(?) - May 1st 1892 - 31st May 1892.
Miss W. Thrift - July 5th 1892 - August 12th 1892.

Assistant Teachers

Miss Mary Bell - 19th April 1876 - 29th June 1882.
Patty Brewer - November 1886 - October 14th 1888.

Monitors

Lavinia Silvester - ? - October 1884.
Edith East - January 26th - April 15th 1885.
Elizabeth Cooper - June 16th 1885 - October 8th 1886.
Miss Ida M Hoskins - October 8th 1886 - October 1888.
Miss Edith Ambridge - October 1888 - October 1889.
Edith Bridgewater - November 25th 1889 - April 14th 1890.
Ethel Luker - April 1890 - before April 1891.
Harriet Selby - About April 1891- ?
Florence Ambridge - June 1892 (Temporary).

Pupil Teacher

Harriet Brooks Selby - About 1891 - ?

Julia Bell, with her sister Mary as assistant, took up residence in the school house in April 1876 and began her work at the school. The first impression Miss Bell had was of children who were very far behind and who would have much work to do to catch up. When the inspector arrived a month later, he felt it best to say little as the new teacher had only just started but he expressed the hope that the next year would show a satisfactory school.

One of the first actions Miss Bell organised was to have a curtain put up to separate the infants from the rest of the school. She was hoping, at the same time, for more equipment, especially reading books.

Attendance continued to be an issue affecting the children. Miss Bell disapproved of parents taking their children away from school to the Agricultural Show in Abingdon and she felt it to be 'very aggravating' when she was trying to get the children 'up to standard'. In November the majority of the younger children were absent from school because the weather was very cold and they had inadequate clothing. Many of the little ones had no shoes to wear and the roads were very dirty. Then came floods in the village, which also prevented the children attending school. The next problem was a measles epidemic, with the children being left with very bad coughs afterwards. There was scarcely a family in the village who was not affected. In the spring, field work kept many of the children away and Miss Bell spoke to the parents without success. A relieving officer, Mr. Fruin, was mentioned for the first time and Miss Bell hoped he would be able to deal with the families whose children were frequently absent. Relieving officers were on the staff of the Poor Law Unions and in addition to their function of poor relief they had responsibility to visit poor families, especially where children had a bad school attendance record. They later were called school attendance officers and played an important role when school attendance became compulsory for children aged 5 to 10 years under the Elementary Education Act of 1880.

The inspector returned in May 1877. Not surprisingly he found the children's results in the examination were as bad as usual. Discipline seemed to be better maintained but he felt it necessary to deduct one tenth of the grant for defective instruction under Article 32(b). This was returned to the school after the managers had written a letter of explanation.

Before the summer holiday Alfred Smewin gained a prize for his scripture knowledge. The Rev. Barber gave small amounts of money to the children according to their attendance during the preceding quarter as an encouragement for better attendance. Within a short time Miss Bell was commenting that they would have had good attendance one day if a girl had not gone to a lottery at the Roman Catholic School in Abingdon without leave and stayed away all day.

After the holidays the head mistress was pleased to receive a log, a box of pens and a box of pencils, having received 12 new slates earlier in the year from the Rev. Barber and some calico and patchwork for practice from Mrs. Martin. Later in the year the school had a new blackboard and two sets of reading books for the upper standards.

The harvest was late in 1877 and some of the bigger boys, aged about 12, failed to return to school until the end of October. When they finally attended, they were troublesome and at times caused disruption to the other children at their lessons. These boys, which included

Isaac Villebois, who left the school the following month, and Alfred Smewin, were obviously keen to leave school and earn a living.

The entries in the log books for the whole of 1877 and 1878 seem to consist of problems with irregular attendance and the behaviour of the older children. Miss Bell was obliged to send one of the children home twice for insolent and troublesome behaviour. Children were being admitted, readmitted, leaving and being absent, sometimes for long periods of time, for 'the most frivolous of excuses'. Martha Pocock and Lucy Villebois were two of the children suspected of staying at home in this way. Ellen Thatcher was kept at home for a month on what Miss Bell thought was the pretence of illness. Later she found out that Ellen had been ill but for the final two weeks she had been at home helping to look after a younger sibling. Poor Miss Bell was very frustrated at not being able to have the children at school long enough to teach them anything.

May 1878 brought the inspector back to the school again. His report was as follows:

> The school has increased in numbers and the attainments of the elder children are considerably improved. The discipline should be firmer. The majority of the first standard are very weak in arithmetic and the infants know very little. The infant instruction must improve or the payments under Article 19B(a) will be seriously endangered.
>
> A cupboard and some maps are needed. One scholar who was returned last year as over six years of age has been struck off the examination schedule under Article 19(b)1.
>
> Grant received £28 . 4 . 0

Lucy Villebois was the child referred to in the above report and after correspondence with the Education Department she was retained on the schedule. The grant for her of 8 shillings was added to the following year's grant.

Mr. Fruin was having some effect regarding the attendance of the children as it was noticeable that liberties were taken when he had not visited for a fortnight. He found that the families were very good at keeping out of his way when he called on them.

In January 1879 the school reopened after the Christmas break with very few children present. The remainder were absent because of coughs and colds and the intensely cold weather. The little ones stayed away for quite a long time because of the inclement conditions and lack of shoes and clothing.

April 1879's inspection was not a happy one. The inspector found the attainments of the infants very unsatisfactory and could not recommend payment of the grant for them. There was a slight improvement in the results of the examination of the older children. Reading was the strongest point but spelling and arithmetic were very weak. The inspector had never met with worse results of a year's teaching in grammar and geography. It is amazing that Miss Bell was able to teach the children anything at all considering the high rate of absenteeism amongst many of the children. Florence Woodley who was eight years old was hardly fit for the first standard due to her poor attendance record.

By the end of the summer term the children were appearing languid and indifferent to their lessons. The harvest was late that year, which meant the four to five weeks of the summer holiday started on August 29th. The children were not told when the holiday would start until the vicar, the Rev. Charles Martin, came into school to tell them on the previous Friday.

After the holiday Miss Julia Bell had difficulty forming a Standard IV as there were no children in that age group at the school. Three of the Davies family had gone to Marcham. James Gibbons was working, as he had passed the 2nd standard and was 11 years old. Ellen Thatcher had left school and gone to live in Kingston. Clara Lay, aged about 12, was seldom in school and Alice Smewin, who was also about 12, was anxious to leave. Edwin Weston aged 8 was away minding pigs for Mr. Stone the farmer and Albert Gibbons was away 'on the same lark'. The latter had been doing this for a fortnight when Miss Bell wrote about it. At the beginning of 1880 she commented that girls as young as six were kept at home for several days to nurse babies. Kate Weston, aged seven years, was absent nearly every morning nursing at home. It was a great hindrance to any progress and very disheartening for those who tried to teach them. In 1880, attendance in school became compulsory for children until the age of 10 and this was raised to 11 in 1893. The Act came into effect rather slowly in some areas but gradually employers found it useful to have employees who could read and write and have some understanding of number work.

The following are the requirements for the six standards from the Revised Code of Regulations 1872, as shown in Wikipedia, the free Internet encyclopedia.

STANDARD I

Reading	One of the narratives next in order after monosyllables in an elementary reading book used in the school.
Writing	Copy in manuscript character a line of print and write from dictation a few common words.
Arithmetic	Simple addition and subtraction of numbers of not more than four figures and the multiplication table to multiplication by six.

STANDARD II

<u>Reading</u>	A short paragraph from an elementary reading book.
<u>Writing</u>	A sentence from the same book, slowly read once, and then dictated in single words.
<u>Arithmetic</u>	The multiplication table and any simple rule as far as short division.

STANDARD III

<u>Reading</u>	A short paragraph from a more advanced reading book.
<u>Writing</u>	A sentence slowly dictated once, by a few words at a time, from the same book.
<u>Arithmetic</u>	Long division and compound rules (money).

STANDARD IV

<u>Reading</u>	A few lines of poetry or prose, at the choice of the inspector.
<u>Writing</u>	A sentence slowly dictated once, by a few words at a time, from a reading book as used in the first class of the school.
<u>Arithmetic</u>	Compound rules (common weights and measures).

STANDARD V

<u>Reading</u>	A short paragraph in a newspaper, or other modern narrative.
<u>Writing</u>	Another short paragraph in a newspaper, or other modern narrative, slowly dictated once by a few words at a time.
<u>Arithmetic</u>	Practice and bills of parcels.

STANDARD VI

<u>Reading</u>	To read with fluency and expression.
<u>Writing</u>	A short theme or letter, or an easy paraphrase.
<u>Arithmetic</u>	Proportion and fractions (vulgar and decimal).

In April 1880 a holiday was given on Easter Monday and the classroom was scrubbed and cleaned.

The following month the HMI report arrived. It was more satisfactory as the inspector felt there had been a great improvement in the instruction of the infants. The older children had made fair progress but arithmetic in Standard II was poor owing to defective teaching of notation. Discipline was in need of improvement. The certificate for Miss Bell was deferred. Presumably this was Mary Bell, the assistant, as Julia Bell was already a certificated teacher.

On May 28th the Rev. Barber presented certificates of honour from the Government to George Comley and Walter Lay. Two weeks later Miss Bell was complaining about how troublesome the pair were and she was probably very relieved when they left a short time later to go to the national school in Abingdon. George Comley left, in order to go to work.

1881 arrived with a very cold start to the year. The roads were impassable and the traffic stopped after several heavy falls of snow. Mr. Fruin was still chasing up the families who seldom went to school and in February he threatened some of the 'irregulars' with summonses.

May 1881 brought another report from HMI It said:

> The results of the examination both of older children and infants are very moderate. Reading is neither fluent nor intelligent. Writing is poor, both as to formation and spellings. In arithmetic the failures are numerous principally owing to faulty notation. The methods of instruction of infants requires revision. Needlework is not satisfactory. The requirements of Article 17(f) and 19(A)1 must be strictly complied with.

> My Lords will look for decidedly better results next year, especially in arithmetic and needlework, as the condition of an unreduced grant (Article 32b).

> The scholar for whom an honour certificate is claimed does not satisfy the requirement of the regulation applicable thereto.

> The issue of a certificate to Miss Bell is deferred for the present.

In June 1881 Edwin Weston left school. He was aged about 10 and had not passed his third standard. The head teacher remonstrated with him but to no avail. This year the school closed for the holidays on August 1st as the harvest was early.

The inspector had recommended a desk of their own for the infants and, in October, Miss Bell thought that the six year olds were doing rather better with their slate work as a result of these being provided. The remaining infants required more attention than she could give them. She wrote that it was difficult to spare monitors who were capable of managing them, as all children required constant teaching. She was worried about Standard II girls who continued to be very backward and were very idle about learning their tables. Her problems were not helped by an outbreak of scarlet fever. School finished early for the Christmas holidays as the building needed fumigating to stop the disease spreading.

The start of 1882 showed no improvement in attendance. Agnes Grainger, aged about 12, had left to go into service without telling anyone and she had not passed Standard IV.

Elizabeth Pocock, aged about 13, decided she was not going back to school. Six children played truant on the afternoon of February 3rd. Miss Bell thought that all these children lacked discipline at home and, as she had tried every means available to enforce more regular attendance, it was very discouraging.

As a change from complaining about absenteeism, the head teacher wrote on February 10th that two standards were learning to work on canvas, also to 'run and darn'.

In April Miss Bell admitted a girl who was over seven years of age but had not even begun to know her letters. The head teacher wrote that Standard I was made up mainly of children just turned six years and those who had not passed their standard. Edwin Weston left school having passed everything in Standard IV. In May, Henry Gibbens, aged about 11, and John Comley, aged about 10, left to work in the fields without permission.

May again brought the inspector's report. He said that the year's examination was very unsatisfactory and that unless great improvement was shown there would be a serious deduction in the grant. Miss Mary Bell was still not able to receive her certificate.

Towards the end of the month Julia Bell reported that the children were 'somewhat refractory from the bad influence out of doors'. She had never experienced unmanageable behaviour like that before but was determined to put it down. She was able to do so without corporal punishment, which she felt had 'but little effect for real improvement'.

In June, Julia Bell gave up charge of the school. She was replaced by Katherine Shaw. Mary Bell also left.

Most of the entries written by Miss Shaw were about children being admitted. Among these were Mary Florence Ambridge, aged just three years of age, Richard Gibbens, between three and four years of age, and Emily Pocock, just four years of age. Attendance was not compulsory for children under five years of age, which resulted in these younger children attending on a very irregular basis.

Mrs. Weston was fined in January for not sending her daughter Mildred to school regularly. She felt this punishment was unfair because Mildred was not well enough to attend and proved this by obtaining a note from Dr. Dixon of Abingdon to prove her case.

Miss Shaw seems to have made a difference to the school and when the inspector's report arrived in May it noted that there was a very marked improvement in discipline and attainment. The work throughout was fair although the reading and spelling of the lower standards needed attention. The diocesan inspector also gave a good report. He wrote:

A great improvement has been made in the religious knowledge in this school. The children now answer freely and intelligently and seem to take an interest in their subjects. Progress has also been made in writing and spelling, the latter still being rather weak. It would be well to encourage the children to use their prayers at home as well as repeat them at school.

The diocesan prize was awarded to Beatrice Hook for her careful scripture paper, with Anne Palmer and Kate Weston being commended.

Head lice seemed to be a problem but it was seldom referred to as such. Miss Shaw wrote about a child being absent for a fortnight because of a bad head. She also recorded that she had to send girls home because their heads were in a most distressing state or because they were very dirty.

The head teacher made a note in the log book on January 18th 1884 to celebrate the fact that E. Pocock had attended school every day for a whole week for the first time in 14 months.

May brought the inspector's report again. This time he felt the school had improved but much still had to be done before the work could be called good. He felt the infants should have object lessons and 'be practised in appropriate and varied occupations to relieve the strain of ordinary lessons and to teach them to observe and imitate'. For the first time, some thought was being given about varying the learning activities of the children.

In June, Lucy Villebois, Matilda Comley and Mary Pocock were old enough to leave school and Kate Weston, Rosina Grainger, Ernest Villebois and Henry Gibbens left because they had passed the required standard.

In September, two boys were very rude just before they left the playground. Miss Shaw wished to punish them and arranged to do so in the presence of the Rev. Arthur Henry Stanton, Curate of Radley, the next day. When they refused to be punished she sent them home. In the afternoon one of the boys took his punishment but the other failed to return. The next morning this boy returned but still would not take his punishment so she sent him home again. At lunch time his mother appeared, was very insolent and said she would not compel him to be punished. On Miss Shaw's suggestion he transferred to a school in Abingdon.

Lavinia Silvester had been a monitor for Miss Shaw but left in October 1884. She had received a salary of 8s . 6d per month. The head teacher then had to rely on three Standard V girls alternatively undertaking monitoring duties. Soon afterwards Miss Shaw hurt her foot and the doctor told her to rest it, which meant the school had to close for a few days. At the beginning of January the following year she resigned from her position at the school.

Her place was taken by Miss M. J. Brewer. Like so many former head teachers she found the school wanted a great deal of 'working up', especially in reading, which she felt was totally devoid of expression. The children could work straightforward sums with no problem attached to them but could not correctly solve those which required intelligent reasoning. The infants had learnt nothing whatsoever about 'form and colour'. The children had no knowledge of casting off when knitting, so she taught them how to finish their stocking cuffs, following which she showed them how to turn a heel when knitting socks. In later years the girls were taught how to cut out a child's pinafore and sew it together. Edith East had become the monitress giving Miss Brewer more time to help children with their work. Later in the year, following advice from the inspector, the head teacher decided that they would practise their stitches on a Monday afternoon, sew their exam work on Wednesday afternoon and knit on Friday afternoon. Later on, again following advice from the inspector, she cut these activities down to two afternoons per week. She felt the six year old boys were the worst at needlework as they had not had experience of it before.

Girls at Radley School wearing pinafores. Date of photograph is unknown.

Miss Brewer was aware of the need to do object lessons with the infants as the inspector suggested. These took the form of lessons on subjects such as, the cat, the dog, the sheep, the ass, spring, spring flowers, the baker, the blacksmith and names of coins. A subject was

53

taken each week and examined in detail using a question and answer format. The following is an extract from *Evans's Object Lessons for Infant Schools* dating from about this time:

The Cat. - Articles required to illustrate the lesson:

Picture of a cat, cushion. If possible the teacher should have a cat before the class.

The Lesson.

What is this a picture of? What is playing beside her? *(Kitten)* What are kittens? *(Young cats.)* Who has some kittens at home? What is this? *(Head.)* What is this? *(Tail.)* Now point out to me the eyes, mouth, ears, &c.

1. THE CAT HAS A ROUND HEAD, SHARP EARS, AND QUICK EYES.

Look at this picture of the cat. What is the shape of its head? Well, I will draw it on the board, now what is its shape? *(Round)* What are these? *(Ears)* Where are your ears placed? *(At the side of the head)* Where are the cat's? *(At the top)* How many ears has the cat? What is the shape of the cat's ears? *(Pointed)* When does the cat move her ears? *(When she hears a noise)* Can we move our ears? What must we move? *(Our heads)* What does the cat turn her ears for? *(To hear better)* What kind of noise can she hear? *(A little noise)* What does that show? *(That she can hear quickly)* What are these? *(Eyes)* How many has the cat? *(Two)* How many have we? Look at my eye. What is in the middle of it? *(A black spot)* What is the shape of the black spot? *(Round)* Now I'll tell you what the black spot is called. It is called the 'pupil.' Repeat it four times with me. Now spell the word 'pupil' three times.

Miss Brewer was keen that the children had plenty of religious instruction and she arranged for the Rev. Stanton to take a class for scripture on three mornings a week. Sometimes the children were taken to church where they were catechised. When the children were instructed in this way they were required to learn the answers to a number of questions relating to their religious teaching and repeat them frequently until they were word-perfect. In early times it was a means of preserving the Gospel narrative, especially amongst children and the uneducated.

The head mistress also started singing lessons, on the tonic sol-fa system. She used the *Hughes Standard Story Books* for reading lessons.

On the 28th January 1885 Miss Brewer had to deal with her first serious act of insubordination when George Lay would not extend his hand for punishment. A short time afterwards Harriet Tuckey was caned for sulkiness and cried out that she would tell her grandmother. At this time there were 70 children on roll and the monitress had left. Miss Brewer was finding it increasingly difficult to teach the whole school single-handedly and was hoping for a pupil-teacher to join her. A unique situation occurred on May 11th when all the children were present in contrast to May 26th when only 20 children were in school. Some children were suffering from measles and others were watching a procession.

The inspector was not pleased with the falling attainment of the children in May 1885 but felt he could not blame the new mistress as she had only been there a short time. The diocesan report in July was more favourable and the school was complimented on religious knowledge teaching. The inspector felt the subject had been carefully taught and the children had answered the questions satisfactorily. Robert East received the diocesan prize and Arthur Gibbens, Walter Gibbens, George Lay, H. Tuckey and E. Smith were commended.

Miss Brewer was helped in June by Elizabeth Cooper commencing her work as a monitress. John Comley, aged about 13, became a half-timer, which he was allowed to do as he had passed the 3rd standard. He finally left at the beginning of the summer holidays. The head mistress had problems with children coming to school late and wrote that they were 'incorrigible'. The main culprits were the Weston and James families. The school utilised the top part of the playground for teaching out of doors in July 1885 as the atmosphere in the school was unpleasantly warm and enervating.

In September 1885 Miss Brewer recommenced the plan of giving the children homework, chiefly spelling, as this subject in the upper standards left a lot to be desired. She was very happy with the singing lesson and began writing sol-fa syllables on the blackboard as the second and third divisions could sing correctly from the modulator. Nearly the whole of the second division could tell what notes were being played or sung upon hearing them twice. This was the minimum standard required from the more advanced children of the second division by the Revised Code of Regulations, issued annually by the Government's education department. Miss Brewer closed the school for half a day to enable her to go to Culham College, a teacher training college a few miles south of Radley, where Mrs. Tupper-Carey was giving a talk entitled 'Singing from note', which she called the 'tonic staff'. Miss Brewer thought that it would not be as successful as tonic sol-fa.

The head mistress continued to have problems with the bad behaviour of some of the children and had to punish three boys for breaking a bough of the tree in the school playground after being told repeatedly not to swing on it. She had to punish some boys for calling each other rude nicknames. One boy, Walter Gibbens, continued with the practice and refused to be punished. He threatened to leave school if he was but this just resulted in his being more severely punished later. He promised he would not be rude again. Miss Brewer punished the children by keeping them in to work, which she thought was far better than corporal punishment. As time went by she felt the behaviour of the boys was improving and they were showing a greater interest in their studies.

In November Miss Brewer realised that some children had started to bring their lunches to school to be eaten there. There was a rule that they were required to sit down to do so, but on one occasion some girls were playing near the teacher's desk and knocked over an inkwell, which allowed the contents to go through a slit in the teacher's desk. The registers, contained in the desk, were well blotted but some of the entries were illegible as a result. The girls were punished for their carelessness and disobedience.

In January 1886 the school acquired a new set of copy books, the *Holborn Series*. Snow on the ground was causing problems with attendance and Miss Brewer was trying hard to teach the children how to improve their writing by using the blackboard to point out faults. She was also putting greater emphasis on learning tables. She felt Standard II had forgotten much of what they had learnt in arithmetic and this was particularly true of Tryphena Leach.

During February mission workers spent two weeks visiting the church. Miss Brewer left the school in charge of her sister, a former pupil teacher, while she attended some of the services. The children also attended church one morning to hear an address by the Rev. Cyril Bickersteth.

Ringworm became a problem with some of the children. The vicar, the Rev. R. J. Wilson, advised Miss Brewer to tell those affected to stay at home until it had cleared.

Two boys, Harry Grattan and Arthur Gibbens, had to be punished for fighting in February. Miss Brewer, who had hoped that she had succeeded in eliminating this bad habit, was disappointed. The boys later promised to be friends. The school at this time was made up of 18 infants, 13 children in Standard I, 8 in Standard II, 8 in Standard III, 6 in Standard IV, 5 in Standard V and 1 in Standard VI. These were the children to be presented to the inspectors for examination. There were about 11 children who were not in these categories as they were probably infants under five years of age.

Repetition was an important teaching method in the school and Miss Brewer wrote out in the log book the lines to be learnt by the children in each standard:

> Standard IV, V, VI - Extract from *King John, Act IV*
> Standard III - *The Inchcape Rock* by Southey
> Standard II - Last eleven verses of *The Inchcape Rock*
> Standard I and Infants. - *The Sparrow on the Tree*

April and May 1886 brought the inspections once again. In the diocesan report it was stated that the children had passed the religious knowledge examination very satisfactorily, their answering being fluent and general. The inspector thought a little more care might have been taken to ensure distinct recitation among the infants and the older children should have been taught a greater variety of written subjects. Ada Pocock was awarded the diocesan prize. Lucy Rhodes and Martha Belcher were commended. During the HMI inspection, behaviour was found to be very good and the children passed reasonably well in the elementary subjects. Needlework was judged to be fair and music very satisfactory.

In May there was a greater number in attendance than there had been since the school was opened: 72 in the morning, 73 in the afternoon. A 10 year old boy, William Sapworth, stayed away that afternoon as he had been fighting and was afraid of being punished. Miss Brewer sent one of the older boys to the station to find him but he refused to return. Later she went to find him herself and took him back to school to be punished. A few days later she wrote that there had been no trouble whatsoever with the big boys of the first class such as she had the year before; swearing, fighting, calling nicknames, insolence had all been put down at last and she hoped for good. Attendance fluctuated and was low on 14th May as several of the boys spent the afternoon doing 'gents' luggaging'. This consisted of carrying the students' luggage from Radley College to the station and earning a small amount of money.

By the middle of 1886 Miss Brewer was receiving help from a second monitress who worked with the infants. The other monitress helped with Standard I while the head teacher taught the other standards.

There was an outbreak of whooping cough and colds in June 1886. The same month Miss Brewer had a note from a parent, Mrs. James, saying that two of her children had 'blister pox' (sic). She wanted to know whether the other children in the family should attend school. The head teacher said they should stay at home until all signs and symptoms had gone from the house, as she understood it to be very contagious. Three of the Didcock family were sickening with it and also had to stay away as they lived at the same address.

The Rev. A. W. Malim, who married into the Badcock family of Radley, one day gave the children a singing lesson on the modulator. The atmosphere was oppressive and the children were not as lively and energetic as normal although some boys had to be punished on that day for swinging on trees overhanging the farmer's field, in which he allowed them to play cricket.

In July the school received a visit from Miss Crook, mistress from Dorchester School, Miss Coombes of Burcot School and Miss Heevil. The children had their end-of-year party in Radley College's gymnasium.

There was a delayed start to the autumn term as the harvest was not complete. Miss Brewer started using *'Ledsham's Occupations Cards'*, which she felt would be very useful in teaching form and colour.

The school was averaging over 60 children and it was thought necessary to appoint an assistant teacher in order to prevent a reduction in the grant. Miss Patty Brewer, sister of the head teacher was appointed, under Article 84, subject to the approval of the inspector. For the month of December that year she earned £1. Her sister as head teacher was earning £4 . 11 . 8 per month.

In November the school received some new copy and exercise books from Moffatt and Paige. The new exercise books had slates on the cover (a preparation having been put on the cover to make it act as a slate), which were useful as serving in the double capacity of slate and book. The children were provided with slate pencils (wooden handle and metal tip). They brought one penny each to school, for which sum they were supplied with pencils for a year.

January 1887 started off very cold with absences on account of the weather. Miss Brewer adopted a strategy of keeping in, after school, the children who had been away more than once, in order for them to do some school work. Now that she had an assistant teacher, she was able to leave the upper classes and teach some model lessons with the infants, for the guidance of the monitress. There was no Standard VI this year as all the children in Standard V had passed the examination. The two remaining in Standard VI went into Standard VII.

The HMI report for 1887 was good, the school was awarded the merit grant and Miss Brewer received her certificate. She referred to this, when it arrived, as 'receiving my parchment'.

In June the head teacher wrote:

> The first class (Standards III to VII) are getting on well in their work. Standard V began fractions today and Standard VI - division of decimals. We have read through one of the *5th Standard Readers* and are well on the *2nd Reader*. Standards IV to VII are grouped together for reading, using
>> 1) *Fifth Standard Comprehensive Reader*
>> 2) *Hughes Standard Story Book for Standard V*
>> 3) *History Reader Part IV*
>
> I find the plan of grouping suggested by HMI to be more advantageous than the one I used hitherto of each standard reading its own three readers.

Miss Brewer decided to award marks to each page of copy writing and found it was a great incentive to the children to improve the neatness of their work. She awarded a prize at the end of term to the one who obtained the most marks.

June 1887 was a special year throughout the country as it was Queen Victoria's Golden Jubilee. The parks in Abingdon were thrown open to the public and the inhabitants of Radley received dinner and tea in the grounds of Radley College. An organisation called the 'Band of Hope', which taught children to be teetotal, had been set up in the village and its members were taken to the Temperance Fete at Headington Hill Park, near Oxford.

In September Joseph Wood, a pupil, decided to leave school but Miss Brewer sent for him as he had neither reached the correct age nor the required standard for leaving school. Elizabeth and Alice Boulter were admitted to the school, having come from the Roman Catholic School in Abingdon. They only stayed one day as they were sent for to return to that school. Early in 1888 scarlatina broke out in the village. Children from families affected were absent for some time by order of the sanitary authorities.

The diocesan report for 1887 was fairly good and the prize went to George Gibbens. Children who were commended were John Walters, Ellen Weston, George Badnell and William James.

On April 26th a concert was held and Maggie Hoskins and Eleanor Smith sang *The Fairy Ring*, which the vicar thought was particularly good. A solo by Edith Grainger, aged 4, was loudly applauded. The former pair sang at the temperance meeting a month later.

1888's HMI report was not quite as satisfactory as the previous year's. It read:

> The discipline is good and the general results of the examination in the elementary subjects are fairly good. The teacher should, however, make an effort to secure more expression in the reading, which is at present too monotonous. More attention should be given to mental arithmetic and writing in the first two standards and the children there should be given copy books. The singing from note is a satisfactory feature of the work of the school. The merit grant of 'good' is recommended but some improvement should be made during the coming year if this payment is to be continued.

Miss Brewer acted on advice from the inspector and ordered new copy books for 'vertical writing' by the children. Following another suggestion by him, she gave an expression lesson on the blackboard. This resulted in an improvement in the children's reading, which had been monotonous and expressionless. She took the first class (the older children) for a Shakespeare lesson, each child taking a part in *A Midsummer Night's Dream*. Adverbs were the subject of her lessons for Standards III and IV. The infants began embroidery on cards. Up to this time the kindergarten had only pricked cards and threaded beads.

Miss Brewer had a reprimand on July 16th. Someone from the Diocesan Education Department had called at the school on June 28th and found only the monitress there asking the children to repeat the catechism. The school was in a disorderly manner and the registers were unmarked. To the satisfaction of everybody concerned Miss Brewer was able to explain that her sister had suddenly become ill and she was attending to her.

The school was photographed on 17th July 1888 and again in August 1895. The cost of the latter photographs was 1s.6d.

Radley School photograph taken outside the vicarage in 1888.

The Woodley family were all absent on 3rd August as their father had been killed on the railway line. These children then had their school fees paid and Mr. Fruin, the attendance officer, called at the school from time to time with the money. On one occasion it was 4/6 and on another it was 4/-.

The school term continued until 24th August because of the late harvest. Alfred Didcock was attending very irregularly and Miss Brewer found he was working on a farm. She sent a note to the farmer, Mr. Fowles, to ask him not to employ children until holiday time.

Ida M. Hoskins had to finish as monitress in October 1888 and Edith Ambridge took her place. Edith appeared to have made up for lost time as previous head teachers were often complaining about her being absent through illness. Her sister Florence, who would later become a monitress too, was also frequently absent. About the same time Patty Brewer, the head mistress' sister, was married. Miss Mary Brewer resigned at the end of December 1888.

Miss Sarah Ann Jarrett took charge of the school in January 1889. Sarah was born in about 1865 in Monmouthshire, the daughter of William Jarrett, an engine fitter. She found the results discouraging after examining the school. The first class had not learnt any of the new rules in arithmetic, and the needlework had not been commenced. The latter was because the former head mistress had not received any supplies.

In May the inspector reported on the school and said:

> The condition of the school appears to have fallen off during the past year but appears to be reviving under the present mistress. The elementary work is fair. The singing is a little weak and should improve if it is to receive the recommendation for a grant another year.

The diocesan report was also received about this time. It said that the religious teaching had been carefully given and the results were hopeful and promising. A wider range of subjects should have been attempted on paper by the elder children and they should have had lessons on the *Book of Common Prayer*. Some of the younger children were inattentive but on the whole they were fairly successful. The prize, a nicely bound prayer book, was given to George Badnell. Commended were Mabel Thompson, John Walters, Ellen Weston, Kate East and James Woodley.

Edith Ambridge, the monitress, was absent before the summer holiday through illness and it was reported in September that she had been dangerously ill. After the holiday she decided to leave through ill health. Edith Bridgewater took her place but only lasted a short time. Ethel Luker then became the monitress.

June 1890 brought another rather unsatisfactory report from the inspector. The children sang well but reading was very poor, handwriting was lacking in style, needlework was very fair and arithmetic was unsatisfactory. The infants, however, were making satisfactory progress. The diocesan report was better. It said that the religious knowledge was, on the whole, satisfactory, the teaching seemed to have been given with regularity and the children appeared to take an interest in it. The answering was good and the writing fair, with the exception of the 3rd standard, where the spelling needed special attention, being weak. The infants were considered to be working quite well. The diocesan prize was awarded to Ellen Weston. Children commended were W. Chandler, A. Topp, Oliver Smith, J. Walters,

Herbert Gibbens and James Woodley. The children were often taken to church, especially for the many Saints' Days when half-day holidays were given. Religious instruction was given in church and school by the Rev. R. J. Wilson, who was the vicar of Radley from 1880 to 1893. He catechised the children and often read morning prayers. In Holy Week the children went to church each day. It was not quite all work for the children, as a magic lantern show was organised for them by Mrs. Thompson of Radley College in November 1890. The children prepared an entertainment for the parents and friends and the proceeds were given to the new classroom fund.

The HMI report of 1891 stressed the need for a classroom for the infants. The inspector also said that some of the dictation exercises were very well done, but arithmetic was still weak and reading was lacking in fluency and intelligence. Singing was creditable and needlework very fair. The attainment for the infants was just passable. The diocesan report as usual was better. The inspector said:

> Religious teaching has been carefully attended to. The scripture subjects were on the whole well known especially in the higher standards. The catechism was very accurately repeated and written out and its meaning was fairly well explained. The knowledge shewn of the morning and evening services was not very extensive but several of the elder children showed a good knowledge of the order in which the several parts came. The repetition on the whole was very good.

> The diocesan prize is awarded to William Chandler. Commended are Oliver Smith, Florence Ambridge, Harriet Hook, Louisa Silvester, Kate East, Bernard Broad, James Woodley, Mark Villebois, Florrie Silvester and Alice Bennett.

From May 1891 drawing was taken by the boys while the girls worked on their needlework. A drawing exam was included in the list of examinations the children took. The infants began using chequered slates.

In October 1891 schooling became free under the Elementary Education Act 1891 and grants were paid by the Government towards the cost of the children's education. It still depended on subscriptions from people who could afford to give money and from time to time the vicar would give a gentle but pointed reminder in the *Parish Magazine*.

Miss Jarratt resigned in April 1892. She was replaced on May 2nd by Miss M. A. Charins(?) who stayed for less than a month. The school was then without a head teacher for the whole of June. During this time, the pupil teacher, Miss Harriet Selby aged about 16, and the monitress Florence Ambridge aged about 12, looked after the school. For the month of July and until the harvest holiday Miss W. Thrift was the head teacher.

The HMI report for 1892 was good. The children in Standard I and II had passed a very good examination but the results for the upper school were only fair. The new classroom for the infants was approved of. The diocesan inspector felt that the results of his examination were satisfactory and awarded the prize to Florence Ambridge. Commended were K. East, E. Gibbens, C. Silvester and Ellen Broad.

In September 1892 Miss Mary A. Tyrrell became the head teacher.

Radley School's former offices (toilets) in 1998.

Chapter 4

The People 1892 - 1898

Head Teachers

Miss Mary Ann Tyrrell - September 1892 - April 1898.

Assistant Teachers

Miss Harriet Brooks Selby - August 1892 - June 1901.

Supply Teachers.

Miss Haycroft - December 1894 for two weeks, July 1897 for two weeks.

Monitors

Edith Ambridge - October 1888 - October 1899 and September 1892 - June 1893.
Florence Ambridge - September 1892 - 1898.

It became a common occurrence that when a new head teacher started, the first entry in the log book contained a criticism of the school. Miss Tyrrell, who took charge of the school in 1892, was no exception. She examined the children in their work and found that only three of them had passed in all three subjects tested and that no attempt had been made to teach anything related to the government examination since the last inspection five months previously. Knitting and needlework had not even been started. She was not happy about the situation. The platform in the infant room also displeased her and she felt it ought to be removed as it was in the way. At least she seemed to be given a good supply of stock and the following gives an idea of what was procured for the school in September 1892.

> 4 dozen slates, 2 boxes of slate pencils, 1 box of chalk, 1 easel, 2 dozen pen holders, 2 dozen inkwells and stand, blotting paper, red ink, black ink, 4 dozen copy books, 4 dozen drawing books, 4 dozen lead pencils, foolscap, 2 short pointers, 1 long pointer, 3 dozen rulers and 4 dozen exercise books.

> 1 dozen *Century Primers of Part 1 and Part 2*, 1 dozen *Atlas Readers Part 1*, ½ dozen *Hughes Stories - Standard III*, ½ dozen *English History Readers*,

2 dozen arithmetic books, 6 dozen spelling books, 4 dozen *Catechisms*, 1 *Conscience Clause*, 1 drill book, 1 mental arithmetic book, *Evans's Object Lessons*, *Mrs. Fielden's Arithmetic for Infants*, *Poetry for the Young* and *Miss Hibbert's Song Books Parts 1-5*.

Calico, print, holland, cotton, needles, thimbles, scissors, wool, knitting needles, dusters, towels, signal and pointer, hair brushes, combs and nail brushes, lesson bags, pencil cases, maps of hemispheres, sand with a tray, 1 modulator and 5 desks.

At the end of the month Edith Ambridge was again engaged as a temporary monitress. She was still living at home at this time and was the daughter of the local station master.

At the beginning of 1893 new infant desks were delivered and the handwriting of the infants improved as a result. Miss Tyrrell seemed to be making great improvements to the school and in January 1893 the organising visitor reported that the school was in better condition than the previous year and highly creditable to the teaching of the new head teacher. All standards were given a good report and the managers were commended for doing their best to supply the school with what was really necessary for use. By this time the children were attending school more regularly. School was free and parents, as well as the country as a whole, were beginning to realise the importance of education. This must have helped considerably with the children's learning. The inspector felt that it was a good school for them to be at. Drawing in the school was considered excellent by the Science and Art Department, and a grant for that subject was awarded. In 1852 the Government had set up the Department of Practical Art, which in 1853 was renamed the Department of Science and Art. This body oversaw the disbursement of government grants for science and art classes and existed until 1899. Miss Tyrrell also introduced geography. Standards I and II learnt about the meaning and use of a map and a plan, the cardinal points and the size, shape and motions of the earth. Standard III were taught the geography of England and special outlines of the world. They also learnt about the local area and neighbouring districts. Standard IV's scheme of work included physical and political geography of the British Isles and Australia. Standard V studied the geography of Europe, both physical and political, longitude, latitude and the seasons.

In April seven children were examined for their labour certificate and all passed. Four of them left the school as a result. Following the Elementary Education Act 1880, children were required to have a certificate to show that they had reached the necessary educational standard before leaving school if they were under 13 years and were being employed. If the employer was not able to show the certificate, he was penalised. The Elementary Education (School Attendance) Act 1893 raised the leaving age to 11 years. It was later extended to 13 years, was raised to 14 years in the Fisher Education Act 1918 and to 16 years in 1972.

The diocesan report for 1893 was very good and the prize was given to Ethel Silvester. Commended were Bernard Broad, James Woodley, Clara Silvester and Ada Denton.

The government inspection of June 1893 complimented Miss Tyrrell on effecting such a change in the school in the seven months she had been there. The improvement in the examination results reflected her vigorous and intelligent teaching and the inspector felt that all children were interested in their lessons. He was very satisfied with the infant teacher, Harriet Selby, for her 'kindly' teaching, but as she had been under 18 years of age during part of the previous year and was not needed to make up the minimum staffing requirement for the school, the higher grant could not be paid. Miss Selby passed fairly but needed to attend to history and music (theory). At the 1901 census Miss Harriet Selby was living with her parents James and Mary A. Selby in Henley Street in Cowley, Oxford. James was a builder's carpenter. Harriet was described as a national school mistress, as was her sister Mary Ann. Three other sisters were teachers. In the 1891 census Harriet, who was then 14 years old and a pupil teacher, was living in the Radley school house with Sarah A. Jarrett, the head teacher at that time.

Mary Ann Tyrrell, the school mistress of Radley, was born in Oxford in about 1860, the daughter of John and Elizabeth Tyrrell. John was a cordwainer, a shoe maker who used a higher quality leather and had probably served an apprenticeship. Mary Ann was a school mistress at the age of 21 in Frome and, after leaving Radley some years later, she went as a certificated teacher to the national school in Marlborough, Wiltshire. In 1893 the Radley school managers offered Miss Tyrrell an increase in salary. She wrote back in her very neat handwriting to say that she could not accept an increase if there were a deficit in the school funds and that she was quite happy with what she was receiving. The letter is reproduced below.

Radley School
April 2nd
1893

Rev'd Sir
May I, through you thank the School Managers for their kind expression of good will, which touched me most deeply? The privilege of working here, & the help & sympathy which one meets on every side are more than compensation for anything I have

done, or can do. I cannot conscientiously accept the kind offer of the Managers should a deficit appear on the balance sheet for the year just ended, or should it appear probable that my acceptance will cripple the School Funds during the coming year. When I came to Radley the Warden allowed me to fix my salary, & it is quite sufficient.

Once more thanking the Managers for their Kind appreciation of work which, no one knows better than myself is full of mistakes & failures,
Yours Obediently
Mary A. Tyrrell.

66

The school bank account was with The London and County Banking Co. Ltd. in Abingdon, and in 1893 the records show that she received £63 . 14 . 6 per annum. The rate gradually increased until, in October 1897, she was receiving about £11 . 3 . 8 per month. At this time the school was having to make regular payments for fuel to Mr. Jethro Silvester of the Bowyer Arms public house. As well as being a publican he ran a coal, coke and gravel business in the village.

Miss Tyrrell introduced 'varied occupations' for the children, which provided more interesting lessons, and she also held pupil-teacher lessons, between 7.30 and 9.0 in the evening, using the *School Guardian Correspondence Class*. In November 1894 she introduced an incentive scheme. After this date those children whose copy books were marked as being excellent on Monday afternoon could do kindergarten pricking and crayon colouring during the writing lesson on Friday afternoon. Also those boys whose drawing was marked as excellent on Tuesday afternoon could do crayon drawing and colouring during the writing lesson. She wrote a syllabus for the infant class, which can be seen below:

Class 1 - Upper Infants

Reading
> *Century Primer Part II*
> *Blackie's Primer Part I*

Writing
> a) capitals and small letters from dictation
> b) name
> c) transcription

Spelling
> names of common objects

Tables
> addition tables

Multiplication
> tables to the end of the 3s

Arithmetic
> notation to 100, addition sums of 4 lines (Nos to 100)

Varied occupations
> a.   ninepins
> b.   drawing
> c.   object lessons
> d.   pricking and embroidering
> e.   paper folding
> f.   recitation
> g.   singing
> h.   crayon colouring
> i.   copy books

Class 2

Reading

Century Primer Part I

Writing

    a) easy words from blackboard

    b) small letters from dictation

Spelling.

    word building (words of three letters)

Tables

    addition table to the end of 3 times, multiplication table to the end of 3 times

Arithmetic

    figures to 100 from blackboard, figures to 20 from dictation, easy mental addition and subtraction

Varied occupations

    a.   ninepins

    b.   drawing on slates

    c.   object lessons

    d.   paper folding

    e.   recitation

    f.   singing

Class 3

Reading

    capitals and small letters printed out or named on alphabet sheets, alphabet blocks and letters picked out

Writing

    a c e l o u d.

    figures and arithmetic

    0 to 9

    counting to 100

    twice times addition table

    twice times multiplication table

Varied occupations

    a.   stick laying

    b.   bead threading

    c.   thread picking

    d.   object lessons

    e.   recitation

    f.   singing

1894's government inspection produced an admirable report. The children in the main school passed well in all respects. The inspector said that the infant children were happy and well instructed and the teacher, Miss Selby, had passed fairly but she should attend to geography, history, music and knowledge of method. Miss Selby had a fortnight's absence in December to sit the Queen's Scholarship Examination, in which she obtained a second class.

The diocesan inspection was equally favourable. The children had passed a thoroughly excellent examination. The prize was awarded to Bernard Broad. Commended were Clara Silvester, Edith Pocock, Lucy Bennett, William Sadler, Fred Smewin, Mark Villebois, Cecil Smith, Florrie Hook, Kate Silvester, Richard Weston, Alice Bennett, William Pocock, James Grimes, George Hook, Nellie Sadler, Albert Willetts, Lily Silvester and John Boulter.

About this time a number of children were sent home because they had 'eruptions' on their heads.

Young children were still being admitted and in June 1894 Arthur Boulter started school, aged three years. Children aged 12 and 13 were also pupils there. Attendance was greatly improved, probably because school was becoming more interesting, attendance for most children at the school was compulsory and parents no longer had to pay. The weather could cause problems, though, and in November 1894 the children were unable to walk through the floods. One day they were taken home on a wagon kindly lent by Mr. Taylor, the farmer.

Just before the children finished for Christmas in 1894 the school closed for the first election of the parish council under the provisions of the Local Government Act 1894.

The Rev. James Okey Nash, when writing in the *Parish Magazine*, constantly sang Miss Tyrrell's praises, especially when she took over the girls' choir when Mrs. Walker was no longer able to continue with it. Miss Tyrrell's entries in the log books were very neat and she must have encouraged the children to be likewise as the inspector in 1895 remarked that the children's paper work was remarkable for its extreme neatness. Spelling was rather weak but maths was worked with great accuracy. All subjects were well taught. The inspector felt that the tone of the school was excellent and he recommended that the highest grant available, under Article 105, should be paid. The diocesan inspector reported that all was highly satisfactory. The prize went to Clara Silvester. Commended were L. Bennett, F. Hook, W. Sadler, W. Pocock, L. Steptoe, M. Villebois, B. Godding, A. Willetts, H. Williams, G. Broad, L. Grimes and Lily Silvester.

In May 1895 the vicar reported that the balance sheet for the school for the previous year showed a balance to the good of £13. He felt it was very satisfactory but there were still some accounts to pay and the expenses would be heavier the following year. He was very disappointed that the alms given at Easter were £2 down on the previous year. It was part to the vicar's duties to instruct the children of his parish in the catechism and they received this on Sundays and during the school week.

May Day was an event which was celebrated in many ways and the following is the vicar's summary of the day in 1895:

> It was a glorious day, almost too hot. Mrs. Dockar-Drysdale invited the whole village for Monday, 13th, and we luckily escaped the wet and cold of May 1st. The children marched down to the sound of their own trumpets to Mr. Betteridge's field. The maypole was resplendent with bright new ribbons. Then came the change of sovereigns. The Queen Dowager was enthroned and speedily deposed by the new May Queen, Lily Silvester. She did not look as if the crown made her uneasy, as the poet says it does, but the most uneasy person was Mark Villebois, the Jack-in-the-Green. After silently enduring the heat for some time, he at last broke loose from his leafy dungeon, and saved his life. The children sang quite a number of songs and plaited the ribbons with wondrous skill. The band then mustered and, once started, played excellently. The girls did credit to Mrs. Croome's teaching of *The Lancers*. Then everyone was called to tea as fast as they could be served. Cricket, photographing, tugs-of-war and general dancing filled up the time to the close of a most happy holiday.

May Day and maypole dancing continued each year until the outbreak of the First World War. The girls mostly wore white dresses and everyone enjoyed the tea, milk and buns which were in plentiful supply. The May Day celebrations were held in a field in the centre of Lower Radley and most of the houses surrounding that area had a stile or gate to enable the residents to enter. Ethel Lay, who died in 2007, just remembered the last such event, held in about 1914, and told her niece:

> There was a May queen each year who was crowned with flowers by the old queen. Both queens were pulled around the village in trucks by the boys. My sister Lily was the old queen and the boys tipped her down the bank. No bones broken though. Millie Weston was the new queen. I was in tears earlier as I came second choice. I well remember Don Mattingley saying, 'Don't fret you will be queen next year'. He was six years old and I was five.

Mrs. Dockar-Drysdale presented the following prizes to pupils in August, at the same time expressing the grateful thanks of the village to Miss Tyrrell, Miss Selby and Florence Ambridge who were doing an excellent job. She felt they had really earned their holidays.

(1) Holy Scripture

Bishop's prize	Clara Silvester
Standard II	Willie Pocock
Standard I	George Hook
Infants	Charles Broad, Lizzie Grimes

(2) Progress

Standard V	Clara Silvester
Standard IV	Ezer Grainger
Standard III	Willie Pocock
Standard II	Nellie Sadler
Standard I	Fred Denton
Infants	Emily Boulter

(3) Conduct

Standard V	Florence Silvester
Standard IV	Miriam Gibbens
Standard III.	Bella Broad
Standard II	Nellie Sadler
Standard I	Sarah Grainger
Infants	Martha Woodley

Prizes offered for special subjects

(4)	Writing and spelling	Lucy Bennett
(5)	Arithmetic	George Woodley
(6)	Needlework	Lucy Bennett, Beatrice Godding
(7)	Drawing	John Topp, George Silvester
(8)	Geography	Miriam Gibbens
(9)	Wild flowers	Lucy Bennett, Kate Bennett
(10)	For holding medals	Ada Gibbens, Miriam Gibbens

Attendance - Possible attendances 417

417 Ada Gibbens
417 Miriam Gibbens
416 Lucy Bennett
416 Albert Willetts
416 Frank Willetts
415 Eli Sadler
415 George Woodley
414 Albert Bennett
413 Richard Weston
413 Fred Denton
412 John Topp
412 Fred Smewin
412 Mark Villebois.
412 Florence Hook

411 George Hook
410 Willie Sadler
410 Ezer Grainger

CATECHISM AND SUNDAY SCHOOL

(I) Attendance - George Hook, Frank Willetts
(2) Answers - Clara Silvester
(3) Conduct - John Woodley

List of Prize-Givers

Mrs. Dockar-Drysdale, Mr. Dockar-Drysdale, Mr. Norton, Dr. Monk,
Mrs. Thompson, Mrs. Croome, Mrs. Titherington, Mrs. Bryans,
Mr. Simpkinson, Mrs. Badcock, Mrs. Walker, Mrs. Taylor, Mrs. Hewer,
Mrs. Betteridge, Mrs. Maslen, and the Clergy.

In August Radley Feast Day took place. The children sang capitally, even though it was the school holiday, according to the vicar when he wrote in the *Parish Magazine*. He thanked the teachers who had given up their holiday time to be there. Little else was written about the feast but in the following year there was mention of the third Berkshire Friendly Club of Radley Feast Day. On this occasion Mr. Walker, the farmer, lent his barn and Jethro Silvester prepared an excellent dinner for about sixty people.

In October 1895 there were 74 children on roll, with three infants absent for the winter. In March of the following year there was an influenza epidemic and an outbreak of ringworm, which caused many children to be absent. Generally, though, the children were regular in attendance. They had been encouraged to attend school by medals and ribbons being given for perfect attendances. Unless there were exceptional circumstances the children would not receive their medal if they missed a day's schooling. The following excerpt is taken from the *Parish Magazine* of December 1895 and is a typical list of winners:

MEDALS FOR REGULARITY, PUNCTUALITY, AND CLEANLINESS

Blue Ribbon for

23 months	Ada Gibbens
22 months	Miriam Gibbens
11 months	Kate Williams
6 months	Willie Pocock
5 months	Nellie Sadler
5 months	Lizzie Grimes.
4 months	John Woodley

72

Blue Ribbon for

3 months   Kate Barrett, Lucy Bennett, Maurice Palmer, Lily Silvester,
                Florence Enser, Louisa Sadler

Red Braid for

2 months   Bella Broad, John Topp, Charles Godding, Charles Broad,
                Percy Badnell, Beatrice Godding, Anna Bennett.
1 month   Alice Bennett, Sarah Grainger, Bertie Pocock, Fred Denton,
                Frank Fulbrook, Bertie Godding, Lavinia Grace, Daisy
                Ballard, Ada Woodley, Edith Sadler.

The vicar remarked in the magazine that the children were much cleaner and tidier in appearance and that the giving of medals depended not just on perfect attendance but also on punctuality and tidiness. He continued that it was very easy to have muddy hands and not all children liked to clean their shoes and have a clean handkerchief. He gave praise to the mothers who helped many children to be able to receive their medals by fulfilling these requirements.

A slight departure from the usual timetable came in January 1896, when Miss Tyrrell introduced story reading to the children instead of the last lesson. She was using *Schedule S* for the scheme of work at this time. This appeared to be something new as it was discussed at the managers' meeting and was considered a serious step to take. The system of inspection had also changed. The school had surprise visits by the inspector from this time onwards. At the same meeting the managers agreed that the cost for the hire of the school would be five shillings for political meetings, dances and concerts and one shilling and six pence for matters educational or part of the regular parish system, such as night school, glee class or lectures.

Mrs. Josephine Dockar-Drysdale, who had become a manager in about May 1895, was interested in the school and presented it from time to time with gifts. These included a set of natural history pictures, five pictures of birds, a map of Europe and the necessary apparatus for basket making. Gifts also came from the manager of the Scholastic Library in the form of books, as well as a gift of ten books from the Rev. Nash. The following year Mrs. Cotart gave 40 pairs of slippers and stockings to the school in order that the children could change and dry their boots and stockings when they attended school on wet days. This was probably in response to the vicar suggesting that perhaps it would be better for the children to go barefoot rather than sit in wet boots all day. When the slippers arrived some of the boys were punished because they took the opportunity to dip their feet into the pond in order to try on the slippers. Unfortunately for them they were seen doing it. Mr. Edward

Franklin Simpkinson from the College, a school manager, had presented a teacher's desk earlier, and in 1896 he gave a work basket, a cupboard for kindergarten materials and a case for a museum. Mr. Charles Taylor, the farmer, was also a manager. For the first time in the school's history, a parent was invited to be a manager to represent the families in the village. He was Mr. James Gibbons.

The inspectors from the Government and diocese had nothing but praise for the excellently conducted school in 1896. They all reported that the children were well taught and the tone of the school was good. They thought that the teachers were encouraged by the fact that the children seemed eager to learn and that they had the confidence of the parents. The inspectors also suggested that the managers apply for a £10 grant given to small populations. The school at the beginning of 1896 was £20 in arrears and the managers were eager to balance the account. Mr. Taylor, Mr. Simpkinson, Mr. Hewer, Mr. Bryans and Mrs. Bryans all contributed £1 to the fund to help offset the loss. The small-population grant, which they received later in the year as the population of Radley was below 500, and the full grant received for good attendance and excellent results made a big difference. The diocesan prize went to Richard Weston. Commended were Miriam Gibbens, Florence Hook, William Pocock, Beatrice Godding, George Hook, Nellie Sadler, Martha Villebois, Robert Godding and Lizzie Grimes.

The monitors from Radley and other schools were rewarded for their work with a day out in Oxford in November. They visited the gold fish at Christ Church College and the deer at Magdalen College. Their greatest treat though was to visit Keble College, where they met the Warden and had tea followed by listening to the music box and seeing the famous picture, *The Light of the World* by Holman Hunt, in the College Chapel.

The vicar in 1896, the Rev. James Okey Nash, used the *Parish Magazine* as a way of communicating with his parish and his comments at times could be quite to the point, especially when trying to get adults and children to attend church services. He knew how to flatter people but he also had strong opinions about certain things. He wrote about the events in school and the following is one of his articles written in November 1896:

Cooking Classes:

Mrs. Dockar-Drysdale is very kindly making arrangements for some lessons in cooking for the elder girls in Radley; and the girls seem eager for the opportunity, for they feel that, whether in their own home or in service, it is a great thing to be able to cook. French villagers are said to be far better than us English at making pleasant and wholesome food at small expense. And somebody once said he believed half the crime was due to bad cooking. (Is this from the husbands and big sons losing their temper and throwing things about, or because they desert their homes and get into bad ways?) But certainly, if from the same material there can come a meal which invites you to sit down and one which makes you want to go away, there is no doubt which is best. Wise housewives understand about this. It is like the difference made by a clean and comfortable, cheerful home, as against an untidy, cheerless home, in the happiness and love and temperance of that household. It is an affair first of knowing, then of thinking and taking trouble.

Just before Christmas 1896 the school had to be closed for five weeks because of an outbreak of measles. Miss Tyrrell wrote that Fred Weston was too ill to attend school and Raymond Mattingley had died, probably not of measles as the vicar wrote that there was one thing they had to be thankful for - they had lost none of their little ones because of measles. In other places it had not been so. He said that if they wanted companions in misfortune then it was that half of England seemed to have been attacked. Even when the children returned, they were not fit for much mental work. The children mainly worked on preparing an entertainment for their parents. After this function the vicar picked out for praise: 'Albert Bennett, Kate Stimpson and the mice, the infants' charming musical drill with nursery rhymes, the girls' topsy-turvey song and the dance they had learnt so quickly - these were some of the best of them'. The boys seemed to be fit enough at the end of the month to carry the luggage for Radley College boys, which resulted in the registers not being marked.

In 1897 Miss Tyrrell wrote that the school year in the future would be divided into three terms, i.e., Christmas to Easter, Easter to Harvest and Harvest to Christmas. At the end of each term a terminal exam would be held and the upper school would be divided into two classes, each of which would again be divided into an upper and lower division. For some lessons specified in the syllabus the sub-divisions would be grouped. This seemed to be the start of a recognition that better teaching could be achieved by teaching lessons more tuned to the age and ability of the children. Composition, or story writing as we would now call it, was part of the curriculum and one of the subjects set was 'How to catch a pickpocket'. The boys were able to play football on a field by kind permission of Mr. Taylor, the farmer, but they were in need of goal posts and a request was made for a benefactor by the vicar in the *Parish Magazine*.

At the beginning of 1897 there was an outbreak of whooping cough and only half of the 67 children on roll were in school. A troublesome cough affected the children who were present and it was decided to close the school for a while. The vicar worried that the children would forget that 2 + 2 = 4 and how to spell 'cat'. Following these problems, several children were absent with ringworm.

The annual report arrived in June 1897 and again it was highly creditable. Praise was given to Miss Tyrrell, Miss Selby and Florence Ambridge. The vicar felt that mothers who had to look after two or three children would appreciate the teachers' difficulties in teaching and maintaining discipline, but he thought that fathers would not understand.

Queen Victoria's Jubilee was celebrated with a whole day's holiday on June 25th and a half day's holiday was given the following Wednesday as it was the date of the parish jubilee treat given by Mrs. Dockar-Drysdale.

About this time there was a movement going on all over the country for a 'Federation of Voluntary Schools'. Most church schools were thinking of joining and organising together. Following a vote at a special meeting of the Conference it was decided that Radley would belong to the diocese unit.

On Ascension Day in 1897 the children attended church to sing the Eucharist at 8 o'clock in the morning and then had a very pleasant outing to Nuneham in the afternoon, just before the much needed rain began.

Autumn 1897 saw a drop in the number of children on roll and it then stood at 53. The diocesan report was very satisfactory and the following received prizes:

> Diocesan Prize. William Pocock.
> Commended. R. Weston, M. Gibbens, B. Godding, K. Williams, A. Bennett,
> L. Grimes, L. Silvester, S. Foster, A. Haynes, B. Badnell, M. Woodley,
> R. Godding, F. Enser, K. Stimpson, M. Boulter, A. Pocock, F. Weston and
> F. Badnell.

The attendance on the whole was very good and the vicar, through the *Parish Magazine*, continued to implore the parents to keep it so. He quoted a local magistrate as saying that he never had a case before him from Radley. In fact they were the best school in the district for attendance except for Culham, which was 0.3 points better. Medals were given at the end of the year and there were some impressive achievements. The Gibbens sisters, Miriam and Ada, had never missed or been late for over five years, Kate Williams for three years and Beatrice Godding for two years. Alice and Bertie Haynes and Hannah Hook had never missed since they started school.

The school reopened on January 14th 1898 with Miss Selby, who earned about £5 . 16 . 8 per month, taking charge of the 1st class while at the same time superintending the work of the lower division of the infants, which would be taught by Florence Ambridge. Attendance fluctuated because of the weather and an outbreak of influenza.

In April 1898 Miss Tyrrell resigned her charge of the school. She left a school where the children, according to the diocesan inspector, the Rev. C. E. Adams, 'Answer with great intelligence, are reverent in their behaviour and appear interested in their work'.

The following is the letter Miss Tyrrell wrote in the *Parish Magazine* at the time of her resignation:

My Dear Parents,

Mr. Longland has kindly permitted me to say good bye to you through the medium of the Parish Magazine.

I want to thank you most heartily for the kind way in which you have worked with me during the five and a half years I have lived in Radley. During that time you have earned for yourselves the proud distinction of caring more for your children's welfare than for your own personal convenience. School has come first and the washing days and baby minding days second. I know to what inconvenience you have often put yourselves in order to spare the children to come to school, yet the effort has been made and the children have been sent.

The result is that Radley School and its percentage of attendances is second to none in Berkshire. It rests with you to maintain the high standard to which our school has attained. Please continue to send your children regularly and punctually to school and work with my successor as you have worked with me.

I shall ever regard the Radley children of the present generation as my children, and take a special interest in all that concerns them.

Faithfully yours,

Mary A Tyrrell.

Chapter 5

The People 1898 - 1919

Head Teachers

Mrs. Eliza Jane Holifield (née Ambrose) - 18th April 1898 for about one month.
Miss Elizabeth Broughton - July 1898 - March 1909. July 1909 - July 1910.
Miss Ada M. Harriss - March 1909 - July 9th 1909.
Miss Edith M Welch - September 1910 - July 1920.

Assistant Teachers

Miss Harriet Selby - August 1892 - June 1901.
Miss Mundy - September 1898 - August 1900.
Miss Florence Ambridge - September 1900 - December 23rd . 1903.
Miss Margaret Looker - September 1901 - August 9th 1907.
Miss Moretta Hill- January 1904 - October 18th 1905.
Miss Katherine Watts - October 1905 - ?
Miss Elsie Mundy - 10 September 1907 - ?
Miss Mabel G Moss - September 1910 - April 30th 1917.
Miss Katherine J Moon - September 6th 1915 - November 30th 1916.
Miss P Chaundy - January 1917 - April 30th 1917.
Miss Ida R Rosier - May 1st 1917 - March 1st 1918. Reappointed November 3rd 1919 - ?.
Miss Katherine Violet Cranmer - May 21st 1917.
Miss Dora Goundrey - March 1st 1918 - October 31st 1919.

Monitors

Florence Ambridge - July 1892 - September.1898.
Lily Silvester - June 1901 - ?
Martha Woodley - temporarily.

Caretakers

Mrs. Godding
Robert Godding.

In the *Parish Magazine* of July 1898, the Rev. James Okey Nash wrote:

> After many weeks of seeking, the managers have found and appointed a new mistress to fill Miss Tyrrell's place. Miss Broughton, who has been qualifying for her certificate at Whitelands College, Battersea, will come to us at the end of this month. She has had a distinguished career at the college, having obtained first-class certificates in nearly all the numerous subjects she has taken up. She is therefore a teacher we must all try to help. So we ask all the parents to do what they can to assist her in the education of their children. There are many ways in which parents could most materially assist the school mistress. If they would always uphold her authority. If they would see that at home their children were obedient and well behaved; besides sending them off in time and regularly to school, both morning and afternoon, with nice clean hands and faces. For we want Radley School to be a model school both in learning and happiness, so that whenever the inspector may visit us, he may always report what excellent work we do, and what bright, intelligent children there are in our school to do it so well.

Elizabeth Broughton was born in about 1878, in Sutton, Surrey, the daughter of Samuel Broughton, a gardener.

After the resignation of Miss Tyrrell there was a period of time before Miss Broughton could begin her work in the school as the headmistress. The gap was filled by Mrs. Eliza Jane Holifield. Although in the log book she said it would be for one month, there does not appear to be anyone else between her and Miss Broughton starting in July. Eliza Jane Holifield (née Ambrose) had taught as an assistant mistress in Drayton, near Abingdon, before she married Harry Holifield, a plumber. During the time she was the head teacher at Radley she frequently complained in the log book about truancy and the poor quality of the children's work, which she had to show to the managers. The vicar came in to complain about the boys having dirty boots. Two boys were sent home for being dirty and untidy and one for insolence and bad behaviour. While she was teaching the lower class one week, Lucy Bennett, a pupil, was looking after the upper class.

When Miss Broughton commenced as head mistress, she felt that the children's behaviour began to improve in the first term she was there. She had to send a child home for insubordination but he apologised on his return the next day. The scripture report stated that she was not to blame for the writing and spelling being imperfect. The inspector hoped that the children would be taught a form of private prayer which they could memorise. The prizes were awarded and the following were the successful candidates:

Prize. Kate Williams.
Commended. W. Pocock, A. Haynes, L. Grimes, M. Villebois, P. Badnell,
F. Enser, S. Forster, R. Godding, B. Pocock, M. Woodley, M. Grimes,
E. Hook, A. Pocock and V. Weston.
Radley College Warden's prize was won by W. Pocock.

At the beginning of 1899 there were 64 children on roll. Martha Woodley was absent with German measles and Willie Pocock had gone to a convalescent home in Torquay.

There was a surprise inspection in February 1899 by the organising visitor of schools who wrote that the school had improved overall. The absence of the former neatness of the paper work was compensated by the 'prevalence of greater intelligence'. The teaching methods were sound, and he thought that they should in time 'give rise to a condition of thorough efficiency'. He wrote that the infants were more efficient than at any previous time he had known them. Later in the year, in June, the report was not quite as good as the inspector was worried that the mistress had not yet been able to attain either thoroughly good order or thoroughly good work, nevertheless, a great deal had been accomplished and he had every reason to expect continued progress.

On the 31st March 1899 the school year came to an end and the school was free from debt. The managers had experienced an expensive year because of the many necessary repairs to the buildings. The school income came to £187 . 4 . 11½ and the expenditure amounted to £177 . 3 . 4½. Unfortunately expenses of £6 had to be added on for work carried out during the Easter holidays, which meant that the real balance in hand was £4 . 1 . 7. The Rev. Charles Boxall Longland, vicar of Radley from 1898 to 1916, worried that even that would be swallowed up by drainage problems. In December 1899 the aid grant was £22, the increase in salaries £5, repair of roofs and windows £10 and furniture and new desks £7.

Writing in the *Parish Magazine*, the vicar gave a list of the classes the children were in for April 1899. He wrote that after Easter most of the children would be advanced a standard. The list is helpful in identifying the children who attended the school at this time and is as follows:

THE SCHOOL

STANDARD VI	A. Denton, W. Pocock.
STANDARD V	J. Grimes, G. Hook, C. Hook, M. Wells.
STANDARD IV	C. Barrett, G. Woodley, A. Willetts, F. Denton, M. Villebois, A. Haynes, K. Williams, L. Silvester, S. Grainger, L. Grimes.

STANDARD III	S. Foster, P. Badnell, F. Willetts, B. Pocock, A. Gibbens, E. East.
STANDARD II	A. Bennett, B. Haynes, F. Weston, H. Grimes, A. Betteridge, E. Wells, C. Smewin, F. Badnell, R. Godding, M. Woodley, K. Stimpson, F. Enser, A. Woodley, M. Boulter, L. Grace, D. Scribner, E. East, M. Brewer.
STANDARD I	S. Mattingley, S. Weston, R. Walker, B. Godding, M. Grimes, A. Bennett, A. Pocock, E. Hook, D. Trinder.
INFANTS	G. Bennett, E Denton, N. Grimes, C. Haynes, H. Hook.
1st CLASS	C. Comley, D. Sadler.
2nd and 3rd CLASS	S. Foster, E. Smewin, E. Hook, E. Mattingley, P. Leach, L. Bennett, M. Stimpson.

The total number of attendances possible during the year is 405. The children who have attended school most regularly are:

Robert Godding	405	Albert Willetts	402
Sarah Grainger	405	Kate Williams	402
Kate Stimpson	405	Hannah Hook	402
Ada Woodley	405	Elsie Hook	402
Ada Gibbens	404	Alice Haynes	400
Florence Enser	404	Percy Badnell	400
Fred Badnell	403		

George Hook and James Grimes were able to leave shortly after this as they had passed the 4th standard and had been examined for their labour certificate. Cyril Hook also left the school at this time.

In the summer of 1899 the children enjoyed a school treat and the vicar recorded it in the *Parish Magazine* as follows:

THE SUMMER SCHOOL TREAT.

To Mrs. Dockar-Drysdale our warmest thanks are due for one of the brightest and nicest school-treats we have ever had. On Saturday 22nd July, two large brakes each drawn by a pair of horses drove down to the village green and there our 70 odd scholars were ready waiting. Under the direction of Miss Broughton and Miss Selby they were duly seated, the boys in one brake and the girls in another, and then with many a shout and hurrah away they went to Wick Hall. On our arrival the boys found their way first to the cricket-field, where they watched the victorious Radley XI scoring a victory, while the girls went through the gardens to the park, where the trees gave them plenty of shade for all kinds of games.

At half-past four the children were assembled and, seated in a semicircle, they partook of a splendid tea; silly little grasshoppers that would try to drown themselves in the hot cups, causing no little merriment. After tea the boys enjoyed showing us how to play that strange game known to Radley boys by the name and cry of 'U-erky'! Then some races, which Mr. Norton and Mr. Brown well managed, and when a number of the children's parents had arrived, Mrs. Dockar-Drysdale kindly gave away the many handsome prizes, which the children had won in school and had been provided by the kindness of our many friends.

In the January 1900 *Parish Magazine*, the Rev. C. B. Longland gave a report about the entertainment the children gave on 19th December 1899. He wrote:

The programme which Miss Broughton had so well arranged commenced with an action song, 'Welcome', in which seven little infants showed us how to spell the word. Two songs and two short recitations brought Old Father Christmas onto the stage; his costume was splendid, his basketful of presents, such as children love, called forth loud applause.

Then the grand event of the evening began - 'Oh, the Washing Day' - a musical sketch - well acted and well prepared by six of our big girls and six boys. The devotion of the wives to their washing tubs - and the abhorrence of such discomforts by their husbands - led to such a dispute, so the story went, as to call for the interference of fairy 'Good-Advice', to prevent a disastrous ending to all washing-tubs forever, but fortunately for those who like clean clothes the difficulty was removed, the women promising to take better care of their husbands, and the husbands not to expect too much from their wives on the all-important washing day!

The rest of the programme consisted of songs and recitations of all sorts, but all well done by the young performers! The whole entertainment reflected the greatest credit to the skill and patience of Miss Broughton, Miss Selby, and Miss Mundy.

The start of 1900 saw a very poor attendance, firstly because of the heavy snow, then because of floods. At the end of February a large part of the village was flooded. This happened also in June 1903 and February 1904.

Miss Mundy, who had started as an assistant teacher in September 1898, had a day off for a science examination in May 1900. She was probably an unqualified teacher who was doing her training at the school and taking exams from time to time. She finally took her certificate exam in July 1900 and left soon afterwards. When the school reopened in September of that year, Miss Florence Ambridge had taken her place, under Article 68 of the Code. Miss Ambridge was not mentioned in the log books for two years prior to July 1900 and it is possible that she returned having had some training during those years, as later reports imply. It has not been possible to find out what Article 68 meant but it did not seem to indicate a fully certificated teacher.

The children were given a day's holiday in June 1900 for the taking of Pretoria during the Boer War. This more or less marked the end of the war but guerilla fighting continued for another two years. The children were given a day's holiday when it finally ended in June 1902.

There was a good improvement in the report by the inspector in 1900. He felt the school had made admirable progress and that it had continued in this way under its intelligent and painstaking mistress. He felt the tone was pleasant and behaviour had greatly improved. The neatness of the children's work seemed to have improved once again.

With the increase of national schools across the country over the preceding years, the Anglican church was finding it difficult to fund them all sufficiently and started to look for more help from local subscribers. The cost of running the school was laid out in the *Parish Magazine* for May 1900 as the vicar felt people should know how much it cost to maintain:

> The parents may be interested to know what the education of their children costs. We therefore publish the balance sheet for last year, which ended on the 31st March.
>
> Perhaps some of them would be willing to help the other subscribers bear the expense, if so, subscriptions of 1/- or more a year would be gladly received by either the mistress or the vicar and surely the school has a claim on them for support.

SCHOOL ACCOUNT for Year ending 31st March 1900.

Received.		Expenditure.	
Balance in hand 1899	£10 . 1 . 7	Salaries	£123 . 10 . 0
Annual grant	£76 . 11 . 3	Books, &c.	£ 6 . 18 . 5
Fee grant	£21 . 15 . 0	Apparatus, &c.	£ 11 . 9 . 9
Aid grant	£22 . 0 . 0	Fuel, cleaning, &c.	£ 24 . 5 . 6
		Repairs	£ 12 . 0 . 6
		Rate	£ 0 . 4 . 5
		Other expenses	£ 1 . 8 . 0
Voluntary contributions			
Private individuals	£33 . 19 . 6		
Societies	£14 . 0 . 0		
Collections in church	£ 4 . 8 . 5		
Sale of needlework	£ 0 . 0 . 11	Balance in hand £3 . 0 . 1	
	£182 . 16 . 8		£182 . 16 . 8

At the end of the year the vicar wrote in the December 1900 *Parish Magazine*:

THE SCHOOL.

On Tuesday, 6th November, the school children were examined in their religious knowledge by the Rev. F. E. Robinson, who is the honorary inspector for this district. Unfortunately some of our brightest scholars were obliged to be absent from school that day, still, on the whole, the children present answered the questions put to them well. Mr. Robinson's report is as follows, 'The elder children have been well taught, and they passed a very good examination in religious knowledge though some of the spelling was inaccurate. In the second division the religious knowledge was satisfactory. The infants did sufficiently well. The tone and discipline were very good'.

The Bishop's prize was awarded to Eliza Grimes.
Commended: L. Sylvester, A. Willetts, F. Enser, S. Foster, F. Denton, S. Mattingley, V. Weston, B. Shepherd, R. Walker, F. Badnell, P. Grimes, E. Smewin, D. Sadler, M. Stimpson, and P. Leach.

The growing indifference to religious duties makes it more than ever important that children should learn the great truths of their faith, and we hope the parents of our scholars show their interest in the religious training of their children by

84

hearing them repeat the hymns, &c., which are taught them at school, at home helping them to understand them by such explanation as they are able to give. For religious education, if it is to gain any real hold, must be strengthened and upheld at home.

Queen Victoria died on 22 January 1901 at Osborne House on the Isle of Wight and on the 25th Miss Broughton took the children from Standards IV and V to Abingdon to hear the proclamation of the new king. The children also had a day's holiday to see Princess Christian, the daughter of Queen Victoria, when she came to Abingdon in May 1904. She was there to lay the foundation stone for the new building for St. Helen's School.

Miss Selby's time at Radley came to an end in June when she resigned and took a place at Dropmore School in Maidenhead. Florence Ambridge became the assistant teacher in the infant room and Lily Silvester became the monitor in the mixed department. In January 1902, Florence was allowed to go to St. Barnabas' Infant School in Oxford, which at that time was held in high regard. While she was away Martha Woodley helped Lily Silvester with the infants. The inspector commented in the report of 1902 that Florence had derived much benefit from having been to the school and the children were getting on well under her intelligent and painstaking teaching. She continued under Article 68 of the Code.

The inspector was again pleased at the inspection in 1901. He thought that both teachers were imaginative and industrious and the children were bright and making real progress, with the exception of oral work where there was room for improvement. He also commented that the infants were rather noisy and restless.

In September another teacher started at the school and took charge of Standards I and II. She was Margaret Looker who was previously at St. Mary's School, Marlborough.

The diocesan report for 1901 was good. All departments were very satisfactory. The inspector thought that a larger part of scripture should be committed to memory by Standards III to V and 'The life of Our Lord' should be studied in further detail, as per the *Diocesan Syllabus*. The prize went to Florence Enser. Commended were K. Stimpson, A. Brock, V. Weston, E. East, A. Woodley, L. Silvester, M. Woodley, M. Stimpson, P. Leach, S. Mattingley, D. Sadler, F. East, L. Walker, E. Hook, F. Sadler, and M. Weston.

In January 1902 Miss Broughton, Florence Ambridge and several children were vaccinated, probably for smallpox, and were rather indisposed as a result.

A more unusual excuse for absenteeism was given by Frank East after the summer holidays in 1902. He was not able to return to school until October 13th of that year having suffered from severe sunstroke.

Miss Broughton occasionally had to cane children for being late and send them home for being insolent. Children on the whole, though, were punctual and attended regularly. There was the occasional case of ringworm, German measles, influenza, coughs or colds. Miss Broughton herself seemed to have very little time off school and it was only in March 1903 that she recorded that she had been absent because of illness. The inspector in 1903 thought that she was a most conscientious worker and that she tried to teach intelligently, but unfortunately the results of her efforts were disappointing. Solving problems in arithmetic was exceptionally bad, the children being effectively unable to grasp the meaning of quite simple questions. Handwriting, spelling and composition were poor and though some of the children were responsive in geography lessons the answering was confined to a minority. The inspector hoped that during the coming year the teaching would be made more effective and that the school would be raised to a higher level of efficiency. The infants he thought were methodically and intelligently taught and were being successfully prepared for promotion to the upper school.

The head mistress was again absent in December 1903, when she had an abscess on her face. Miss Ambridge taught the mixed school while Miss Looker taught the infants. At the end of that month Florence Ambridge left. She married Oliver Stephen Smith, a baker working in Oxford, at the beginning of February 1904. Her place was taken by Miss Moretta Hill who was born in about 1880. She was the daughter of Charles and Mary Hill of Oxford, where the family were all born. Her father was a decorative artist/ house painter.

The school report was much more favourable in 1904 and the inspector was happy with the school, although he felt that composition generally, arithmetic in the first two standards and enunciation in reading were the weaker points. The curriculum was expanding and more physical education was included. For three weeks in April, maypole drill took the place of military drill. The report for 1905 was also favourable but the inspector commented that it was difficult for the infant teacher to keep three classes gainfully employed without the help of a monitor, yet she 'kindly managed them'. He felt the head mistress conducted the school with zeal, care and intelligence.

In March 1905 Alice Vasey contracted diphtheria and her brother had to stay at home because he was a contact. Diphtheria seemed to occur sporadically in the school. Esther Foster contracted it in 1907 and had to be admitted to the hospital for infectious diseases. In May 1908 Geoffrey Topp suffered from it, followed very soon afterwards by scarlet fever. In September 1909 Florence, Ben and Bea Wilkinson all had to go to the isolation hospital with the illness. Sylvia Saunders was suffering from it in February 1910 and the following month it was Alfred Comley.

Alice Vasey must have recovered from her illness as she was awarded a certificate at the diocesan inspection later in the year. The awards then were:

Prize. Hannah Hook.
Certificates. Lizzie Hudson, Frank East, Jessie Hill, Kate East, Florrie Enock.
Commended. Priscilla Leach, Edgar Smewin, B. Mattingley, Dolly Denton, May
Comley, Alice Vasey, Florence Gibbens and Jack Stimpson.

On October 4th 1905 Moretta Hill was absent for the wedding of her sister, also a teacher, and on the 19th October 1905, she ended her duties at the school. She was married two years later in Oxford. With her departure the position in the infant class was taken by Miss Katherine Watts from St. Aldate's School, Oxford.

In 1906 the HMI report congratulated Miss Broughton on working with brightness and intelligence and on the fact that the children were happily dealt with and were making creditable progress in most respects, but the knowledge of number in the lower division was not sound and the babies needed to be profitably employed. The remainder of the school and the teachers were complimented for teaching with care and intelligence. It was announced that from April 1906 the school would be called Radley Church of England School. It had taken about four years for the school to lose its national school identity following the 1902 Education Act. The number on roll at this time was 56 with an average attendance of 55.2. These figures changed in June when several children were taken ill with mumps. On June 18th the school was closed on the doctor's orders as the outbreak was quite severe. It reopened on July 2nd but there were still cases in the village.

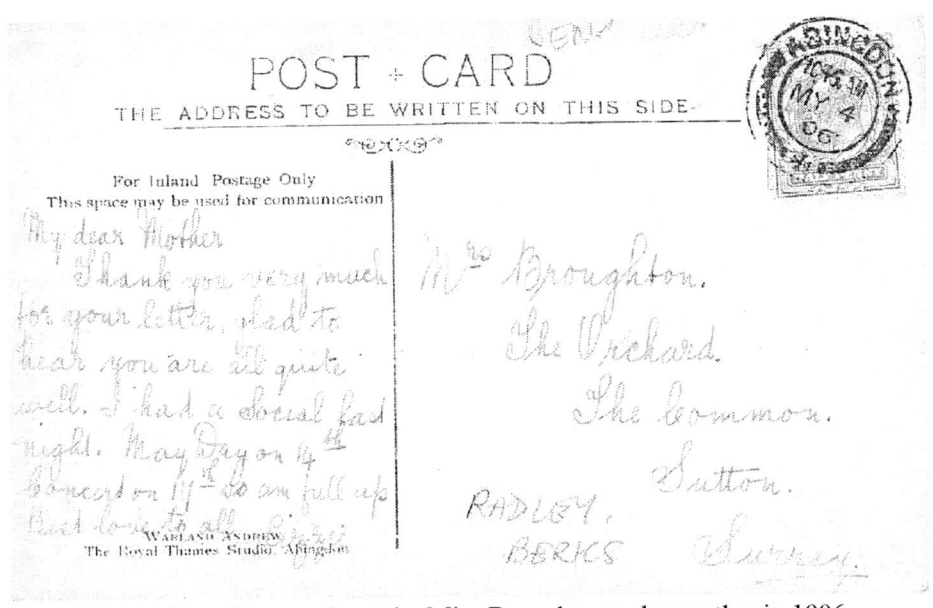

Rear view of postcard sent by Miss Broughton to her mother in 1906

Front view of postcard sent from Miss Broughton to her mother in 1906

The following year, in June 1907, Florence Gibbons was taken to the isolation hospital with scarlet fever, which possibly resulted in her being absent in June 1908 with heart problems, returning later for half-days only. She must have been very young when she had scarlet fever as the log book entry for November 16th 1909 referred to the fact that she was removed from the school books as being under the age of 5. Florence was readmitted in January 1910 following her fifth birthday. The Pocock brothers had to stay at home because they had been exposed to the infection. There was another outbreak of the illness in June 1909 and at least nine children contracted the disease, which was still causing problems to Elsie Stimpson, Nelly Stimpson and Florence Enock in September of that year.

In June the school received its annual report from the inspector. It read:

> The teachers work with earnest and by satisfactory methods. They have achieved creditable success on the whole but the answering of children in oral arithmetic is only fairly intelligent. The needlework and drawing are, however, well done and deserve a special word of praise. Voice training exercises should be given in singing lessons. The order and discipline are good. A continuous reading book is required for the first class.
>
> The reports of the periodical examinations held by the head mistress should be duly recorded and they should be more informing. At present they are so general in character as to be valueless.

The infants are happily managed, carefully taught and are making pleasing progress. Greater variety is needed in the object lessons. As was before repeated, a new decimal ball frame on a stand is required.

During 1907, Mr. Chandler, the drill inspector, visited the school and this seemed to indicate a change that occurred in the type of inspections the school received. This was the first indication of subject specific inspectors visiting the school. A few years later, in 1916, the children were watched by the same inspector and he felt there was an improvement in the 'arms-across-bend' exercise. He commented on the fact that the children had their arms well back in lines. The lower division were examined on turning on heels and toe. With the infants he suggested that the exercises should be taken in a more definite order.

Miss Elsie Mundy took Miss Looker's place as a supplementary teacher in September 1907.

The children were given a treat in December 1907, when a travelling menagerie and museum visited the school. An exhibition was given during the dinner interval. In February the following year the children from the first class (the older children) attended the Corn Exchange in Abingdon to hear a lecture entitled 'Wild animals I have known', by Mr. E. Thompson.

The following is the inspector's pleasing report for March 1908:

> The school is conducted with spirit and intelligence and has greatly improved since my last visit. The upper classes are very well taught, the lower are helped too much. The boys take much interest in their manual work and have done well with the resources at their command, but better equipment is needed. The infants are making good progress. The tone of the school is very pleasant.

Early in 1909 Miss. Broughton was absent through illness and her place was taken by Miss A. M. Harriss, a certificated mistress. Miss Broughton returned to school in July 1909 but in July 1910 she resigned. Miss Edith M. Welch became the new head teacher in September of that year. Miss Welch was born in 1877 and had trained for two years at Whitelands Training College, London. She was born in Battersea and her sister was also a schoolteacher.

Most of the entries in the log book written by Miss Welch were short and mainly about children being admitted or leaving.

At the beginning of 1911 there was a medical inspection and one child was excluded. In February of that year some of the older children attended a lecture at the Corn Exchange, Abingdon, entitled 'A Country Walk'. Lessons on the census were given as it was being taken in March 1911. Some children had whooping cough and others chicken pox or measles. In June 1911 the school closed for a week for the Coronation of King George V. During this year James Mattingley and George Smewin attended the Woodwork Centre in Abingdon. Mick Portsmouth's father, when he was a pupil at the school (1913 - 1922), attended these classes at the council school in Ock Street, Abingdon.

Radley School from the Packer collection of Oxfordshire Photographic
Archives. Date unknown but after 1905.

Berkshire Local Education Authority, in Reading, seemed to feature more often in the log-book entries from 1911 onwards. In February, the head teacher had to send the register to the Board of Education in Reading and in February 1912 she had to forward the new timetable for their approval. It was approved and returned to be copied on to a larger sheet. In February 1913 the annual report had to be sent to them.

In April 1912 Mr. Simpkinson of Radley College, one of the school managers, copied the report from the inspector into the log book. His handwriting was very difficult to read but the general impression was that the school was under effective discipline and the children were very well behaved. The report suggested that children should be in fewer groups for arithmetic and that unnecessary lines of sums should be avoided. Reading was complimented but the children needed some knowledge of the principle rules of grammar. The report continued as follows:

The composition exercises are fairly well explained and handwriting is legible though rather too small in some cases. The errors should be now carefully marked and corrected. History and geography are quite good. The children have a good knowledge of facts and discuss them with intelligence. Object lessons are given on excellent methods and with much success, the children showing much interest and mental activity but the elder children should read from sight more readily. Needlework is well cared for but more mending and making of actual garments should be done. The infants are kindly and patiently managed and are a promising section of school. The upper division is making good progress in two elements and bids fair to become an intelligent and well-advanced class. The early lessons in reading are not very good. In the main the children are doing quite well.

The diocesan inspector thought that the school exhibited all the characteristics of a good church school. Elsie Stimpson won the prize and certificates were given to Fred Aparicio, Ernest Stimpson and J. Stimpson. Commended were I. Topp, G. Foster, M. Comley and the whole class in the middle group. In the infants those commended were D. East, A. Turner, E. Gibbens, W. Pitter, H. Woodley, L. Bannister, W. Gibbens, V. Weston, and E. Villebois.

Miss Mundy had to be absent in September 1912, as there was a case of chicken pox at her home, and Miss Moss was absent for about two weeks after cutting her hand very badly and suffering from shock. Just before the end of the year the school nurse, Nurse Dwyer, was asked to visit two families regarding the state of their children's heads. There was a case of scabies and one of ringworm and those affected were excluded. Scarlet fever appeared again in October 1913 when Frank Pitter suffered from it. Miss Welch described how she suspected scarlet fever in a child when she wrote:

> Leslie Bannister returned to school today after a week away unwell. Muriel is at home suffering from a sick headache. During the morning I noticed Leslie Bannister was not quite well and on examination found that he was peeling about the neck and chest. Both the boys were immediately sent home. After a doctor had seen them this afternoon, they were taken to the isolation hospital with scarlet fever.

Leslie and his siblings had lost their mother the previous year and had been staying with friends. In May 1915 the school had to be closed for three weeks because of an outbreak of measles, which affected most of the children. Nurse Dwyer attended the school when it reopened and excluded one child with a 'verminous head' for the fifth time.

At the beginning of 1915 attendance was low because of colds, coughs and 'flu. The head teacher was absent from February 24th to March 5th with influenza and the HMI inspection was cut short because of this. The inspector reported that:

The upper part of the school is in a generally satisfactory condition that reflects credit upon the head mistress. The work in her class however undoubtably suffers from the lack of firm enough teaching in the lower standards when the teacher fails to hold the attention of her scholars.

The infants are in very good hands and are making excellent progress.

In October Mrs. Moon, one of the teachers, was earning a salary of £40 per year. The following month the managers decided that they could not approve a pay rise for her as there was no indication that she was studying with a view to improving her qualifications.

An awareness of the impact of the first world war was shown in November 1915 when the head teacher reported that until further notice, because of the need for economy, the afternoon school would start at 1.0 p.m. There would be a five-minute break at 2.10 p.m. and children would be dismissed at 3.15 p.m. Mr. Silvester delivered the coke and coal for the school and he complained in February 1916 that he had not been paid. He also delivered 6 loads of gravel, probably for the playground, for which he was paid 18 shillings. In August of that year the school was advised to stock up on coal as many miners had joined the armed forces, which resulted in a shortage of men in the coalfields. Four girls were knitting socks for soldiers with the wool Mrs. Dockar-Drysdale had sent in. The children were treated to a magic-lantern show one day and the 11 shillings collected was sent to the Daily Telegraph Christmas Pudding Fund for soldiers fighting at the front. Sixty-four men from the village fought in World War 1 and their names are written down on a plaque on the back, inside wall of Radley Church. Of these, eight lost their lives and their sacrifice is also recorded. No account is given of those whose health was badly damaged by the war nor what effect it had on families who had members away from home. Albert Bennett and Edwin Mattingley, who have been featured earlier in this book, were among those killed.

Caning was still the method of punishment for boys in 1916. Ernest Villebois was caned for throwing stones at the hawthorn bush and cracking the lobby window. Walter Turner was caned for throwing at the walnut tree.

Two teachers left the school in April 1916. Miss Moss was appointed assistant teacher at the Boys' C. of E. School in Abingdon for the period of the war and Miss P. Chaundy, who had only been at the school since January, tendered her resignation. She had been unable to find suitable lodgings near the school and travelling from Headington had 'mitigated against her success at Radley'. In her letter of resignation she said that she found the work at Radley 'a greater undertaking than she expected'. A year later Miss Cranmer, who lived at 56 Hill View Road, Oxford, tendered her resignation at Cassington School in order to accept a position at Radley. She wrote to the managers at Radley to say that her railway fares to their school would be in excess of what she had previously been paying, which in effect would make her salary less. She had been paid £45 per annum at Cassington. Berkshire Education Committee replied that they could not pay for rail fares but they were able to arrange a war bonus of £7 . 10 . 0 per annum for her and Miss Rosier.

There was an epidemic of mumps at the end of 1917 and the school closed early. At the beginning of the next year there was deep snow in January and the resulting low attendance failed to improve before the end of February. At the end of 1918 the school closed for about three weeks because of an influenza epidemic. The following year there was a measles and whooping-cough epidemic and in early 1922 there was another influenza outbreak. The school was informed that the caretaker should be paid for any school closure resulting from an epidemic, but it was his responsibility to disinfect the school before the children's return. A list was given to him of the work he was expected to do and the following is a summary of the tasks:

Cleaning after infectious illnesses

Offices and pails scrubbed and cleaned and walls lime-whited.
Towels, dusters, etc. washed.
Cloakrooms washed and wiped over with paraffin.
Desks wiped with paraffin as water damages the wood.
Manuscript books used by children with infectious illnesses to be burnt and other books dusted.

In September 1918 the children had a half day's holiday to pick blackberries and during that time they picked 17½ lbs.

An interesting event took place for the children on June 26th 1919, when the school closed for the day. The older children went to Oxford to see Sir Douglas Haig on his way to the Town Hall to receive the freedom of the city. Haig was one of the war generals and had studied at Brasenose College, Oxford, before going to Sandhurst. He became the Commander-in-Chief of the British Expeditionary Force and later led the army to victory in the war but not before many thousands of men had been killed. Through the kindness of the headmaster of St. Philip's and St. James' School, Mr. Dent, Radley children were allowed to stand with his boys in the High Street, where they were all lined up. Two days later was 'Peace Day' and all the shops in Abingdon were closed. Many of the children wanted to go shopping on that Saturday but with the shops closed they were allowed to leave earlier than usual on the Friday in order to shop then instead. The Rev. Charles Stanley Phillips was the vicar at this time having come to Radley in 1916. He left in 1921 and was replaced by the Rev. Edward Heseltine Liddiard, who was there until 1928.

Between about 1913 and 1922 the late Ethel Lay (née Stimpson) was a pupil in the school. In the late 1990s she gave some recollections of her time spent there to her niece, Maureen Jeacock, who kindly allowed them to be used in this book. Ethel said:

> We had a happy time at school. The leaving age was 14 years. There was a porch where we hung our coats and lunch bags, an enamel bowl of rain water to wash our hands and a roller towel to dry them. The water always stank and was full of mosquito larvae. The playgrounds were gravelled. There was a walnut tree, which I have noticed is no more, two sycamores and one hawthorn tree in the playground. The lavatories, which we had to call offices - 'Please miss may I go to the office?'- were the usual wooden seats with zinc buckets beneath. Newspaper was used for toiletry. Mrs. Godding and her son were caretakers.

> There was a coal fire in the infants' room with a fireguard. The teachers used to eat their sandwiches there in the winter. In the large room there was a big, round coke stove. Most of us took sandwiches to school. In the winter we laid our bread on the top of the stove to toast. We took enamel mugs and for a half penny we could have cocoa which the governess had made.

> Morning school started with the monitor ringing the bell. We then had prayers and RI (religious instruction). We then had PT (physical training) - no shorts and plimsolls for us - just arms upward stretch, knees bend, etc. It wasn't very easy with all the petticoats we had to wear. We all wore stockings with elastic garters and boots. The boys' boots were always hobnailed. We were all taught reading, writing, arithmetic (maths was not heard of then), geography and history. The boys did drawing and painting and the girls needlework and knitting. An inspector came round once or twice a year to test our work. Writing was my worst subject. It still is. I still have the prize I was awarded when I was about nine for the best behaviour in and out of school. Of course I was then known as 'teacher's pet'.

> We had lovely games, climbing trees, making mud pies, blackberrying, no real mischief.

> A threshing machine with a big steam engine came to the village to thresh the ricks. People brought their dogs and boys brought sticks to kill the rats and mice as they ran about. There was plenty of screaming from the girls as the rats and mice came towards them. Some of the boys would put mice in their pockets and chase the girls with them.

In July 1919 Miss Welch resigned her charge of the School.

Chapter 6

The People 1920 - 1939

Head Teachers

Mrs. Rosalie Marion Gardiner - September 18th 1920 - October 30th 1925.
Miss Elsie Dora King - September 25th 1916 - October 23rd 1916. (Temporary)
Miss C. D. R. Caudwell - January 1926 - April 1927.
Miss Mary Alice Pusey - May 1st 1927 - October 31st 1930.
Mrs. Agnes Frances May Smith (née Pendleton) - November 3rd 1930 - 30th
April 1939.
Dorothy Bevan (Temporary head) - May 1st 1939 - June 30th 1939.
Mrs. Hicks (Acting head) - November 1st 1925 - January 10th 1926.

Assistant Teachers

Miss Katherine Violet Cranmer - February 12th 1920 - July 31st 1929.
Miss Elsie Dora King - May 1st 1921 - August 31st 1927.
Miss Florence Middleton - October 1st 1927 - July 1971.

Supply Teachers

Mrs. Reynolds (uncertificated) - September 7th 1927 - ?
Miss Norah Fairthorne. (uncertificated).

After Miss Welch, the next head teacher was Mrs. Rosalie Marion Gardiner who took charge of the school from September 18th 1920. She was the mother of Tom Gardiner who became the coroner for Oxford. Because there had been a death in her family Mrs. Gardiner was absent from the start of term until October 23rd. Mrs. Elsie Dora King took her place but as she was unable to be there during the first week the children had an extra week's holiday. The diocesan inspector was pleased with what he found in the inspection the following May and felt that religious teaching was given the place it deserved. The prize was given to Florence Pitter and certificates were presented to Cecil Atkins and Lilian Stimpson.

In February 1920 the drill inspector visited the school to demonstrate the new drill syllabus issued by the Board of Education and the following year there was the first mention of a woman inspector when, in February 1921, the instructress of infant physical culture inspected the infant class. A week later a lady from Berkshire Education Committee visited the school regarding the arrangement of central classes.

There was a visit to London in July 1921, when the head mistress and ten boys travelled to their destination by charabanc. This excursion was under Article 44(b) of the Code. In September some of the older children were taken to Southsea for the day, while there was no school for the remainder.

The school was closed on February 28th 1922 for the wedding of King George V's daughter, the Princess Royal, to Viscount Lascelles and again on April 26th 1923 for the wedding of the Duke of York, the future King George VI. The children had already experienced the school's closure for two weeks in February 1922 because of an outbreak of influenza. There was another epidemic of the illness in March 1925.

The HMI report for 1924 was more a commentary on the social conditions of the school than on the education of the pupils. It read:

> 1. The three teachers work well together and work hard. There has been in consequence a very distinct improvement in the work in each of their classes in the last two years.
>
> 2. The school contains two distinct types of children.
>
> a)   a rather intelligent type with plenty of ideas; the attainments of these children are quite good and their work reflects much credit on the teachers.
>
> b)   there are also some very dull children in the school; these are not naturally of low calibre but from poor home conditions or for some other reason they are hard to teach. The teaching given to these children is good, but in spite of the attention paid to them the results are somewhat disappointing.
>
> The brighter children seem in the majority in the two lower classes and there seems a prospect in consequence of a progressive increase each year in the standard of work in the top class.

The diocesan inspector was convinced that the school was one which exercised an excellent influence on the children.

As a result of the general strike and consequent stoppage of trains in May 1926 the head teacher, Miss Caudwell, who had taken over the running of the school in January of that year, was unable to get to the school before 9.40 a.m. one morning. The girls could not go to their cookery lessons in Abingdon for two weeks running. Miss Caudwell seemed to be absent on many occasions through illness, often two days a week, and finished her time as head teacher in April of the following year. Shortly before she left, the diocesan inspector visited and thought that there was a delightful tone in the school. He thought that a daily record should be kept, showing the subject and aim of each lesson together with the number of the main heading under which the lesson came. He wanted the upper class to use their notebooks to compile a summary of the doctrinal teaching, which they could take home with them when they left school. The Bishop's prize went to Bessie Steptoe and certificates were given to Ruby Portsmouth and May Pitter.

Miss Mary Alice Pusey took charge of the school in May 1927, with 42 children on roll. Many of these were absent in June when an epidemic of mumps was in the village. Miss Pusey opened the school to the parents from 2.30 to 3.30 in the afternoon of July 26th and the children gave a little programme of songs and dancing, after which the parents inspected the specimens of handiwork and pastel work to be exhibited at Abingdon Horticultural Show.

Radley School in the 1920s

In July 1927 the head teacher introduced a scheme for individual work for the 11+ children in preparation for the next term. She felt the scheme promised well.

Florence Middleton joined the school as an assistant teacher in October 1927. She had held this position for 44 years when she retired in July 1971. During this time, mainly in the early years, she was frequently absent. She seemed to suffer badly from migraine, headaches, chills, sickness and bilious attacks. In May 1933 she underwent a course of treatment in

Oxford to try to 'overcome her weakness' but she was still frequently absent for a few years after this. When she was absent, a supply teacher might teach the class but at other times senior girls took charge. In spite of all this she was probably one of the most loved and respected teachers who has been at the school within living memory. All the people who were interviewed, who attended the school while she was there, commented on how delightful she was. Her health certainly improved as she became older and there were far fewer absences in later years.

The Buckinghamshire, Berkshire and Oxfordshire musical festival took place in May 1928 and Radley School gained 2nd prize, only missing the 1st prize by one mark. They also gained prizes in handwriting, knitting and handwork at the Abingdon Horticultural Show. In the musical festival of 1929 they were 2nd again even though they were competing against much larger schools. In 1930 they managed to achieve 1st prize. At the start of September 1929 there were only 40 pupils. Miss Cranmer, who had been an assistant teacher since February 1920, finished at the school, which left just Miss Pusey and Miss Middleton. Both teachers were musical and this was reflected in the success of the children. In the HMI report for 1930 there was nothing but praise for these members of staff.

It was about this time that Don Jones, the son of a Radley station master, attended the school. He remembers that the school had two teachers. One was Miss Pusey, the head teacher, who lived in St. Peter's Road and was the only person in that area who had a telephone. The other teacher he remembers was Miss Middleton, who lived in Radley Road and also gave piano lessons. She rode her cycle everywhere and could often be seen feeding the wild cats around Daisy Bank. There were only three boys in Don's class when he attended the school. One was Trevor Lane, who lived next door to the present Radley Post Office, and the other was Donald Steptoe, who in 1940, when he was still in his teens, tragically died of meningitis. The vicar paid tribute to him in the *Parish Magazine* by saying how much his cheerful disposition and high character would be missed.

Physical education began to play a greater role in 1930. Miss Ash, the Board of Education inspector, suggested that the children should have a short period of physical exercise each morning. Netball posts were given to the school and erected in the boys' yard in order that the girls could play netball while the boys were playing football in the meadow. Mrs. Stevenson of Radley College presented the school with 20 pairs of rubber soled shoes for playground PT. In 1933 the physical education inspector reported a great improvement in the class work and physical training of the children and she commended the teachers. The school received three lengths of rope, six small hoops, one wander ball and six tennis balls in 1934.

In January 1931, four boys broke a school window. As they were playing football in a part of the school yard where they were not allowed to go and having been warned previously, the school managers decided that these children must each contribute 4d towards the cost of a new window and 1s . 4d was handed to the vicar, the Rev. Jackson. Later in the year he received 666 farthings, which the school children had collected for the diocesan fund. In 1934 they collected 694 farthings, and in 1935 it was 810.

Mary Shayler attended the school between 1928 and 1935 and she kindly gave an interview to help in the compilation of this book. She remembers the head mistress, Miss Pusey, living in the school house with her cats, one of which came to the school regularly and lay in front of the fire. The children had to go home for lunch as there were no school dinners. Mary sometimes took a sandwich and Miss Pusey made cocoa for the children. Miss Middleton looked after the infants and Miss Cranmer was there for a short time. Each day started with prayers and work was done in notebooks with scratchy pen nibs and ink from the ink wells. Miss Middleton always read a story to the infants at the end of the day. Children almost always went on their own to school from the earliest age, skipping on the road or spinning tops as they went. One day a bolting horse came charging down the road and an older boy threw Mary out of the way of it. Mary remembers that the children were frightened of the school-board man. If children were absent for half a day he was on the doorstep asking why. She also remembers inspectors coming occasionally to look at the children's books.

Radley school children in 1928/9. Mary Shayler is the third from the left on the front row. Miss Pusey's cat is also in the picture.

The diocesan report for 1931 was very good and the following children received awards:

> Bishop's prize - J. Winter.
> Certificates - Dorothy Turner and Owen Cato.

In July Owen Cato was awarded a certificate of merit for his essay 'The Life Boat Service'. The children often attended church and special services included the Purification of the Blessed Virgin Mary, Holy Eucharist, Ash Wednesday, St. Peter's Day, St. James' Day, St. Matthew's Day, St. Michael and all Angels' Day, St. Luke's Day, St. Andrew's Day and All Saints' Day.

The 1932 report was equally good and the following children were given awards:

> Bishop's prize - Dorothy Turner.
> Certificates - Herbert Hambridge and Greta Tubb.

> The work of Trevor Lane and Mary Pearman, both aged 8, was praised.

By 1932 the older girls were attending cookery classes in Abingdon. In February of that year Miss Drew, the cookery teacher, notified Radley's head teacher that she could only take 20 girls in the cookery class. As a result of this, Betty Tubb had to stand aside until the next term to allow Dolly Turner to attend. Dolly, who had returned to the district to resume her studies, was 13 years of age and was the senior girl.

In the afternoon of November 2nd 1932 the head teacher had to attend to Edwin (Teddy) Weston, who had hurt his arm when he fell off a tree in a neighbouring field. She sent Roland Barguss to Teddy's mother, telling her to meet the bus at the bridge and take the child to the doctor. In the meantime she sent a message to the vicar. After opening school and marking the registers, she attended the boy and arranged for him to be seen safely on the bus passing the school at 1.30 p.m. in order to hand him to his mother. Dolly Turner cycled with the bus and returned after seeing the mother join the bus. He had broken his wrist.

Eleven children were entered for the Fry's writing competition in December 1932. Three won packs of 24 picture stamps valued at 2/- each.

During February 1933 a lady called at the school to discuss the 'Milk in Schools' scheme. After trying the 'Cow and Gate' and 'Ovaltine' samples amongst the children and meeting with no response for these schemes, the head teacher discussed the value of milk. Only one child made any attempt to buy milk. The parents were unable to supply a halfpenny to a penny a day for such extras.

In March 1933 there was another diocesan inspection. The inspector saw problems with teaching such a variety of ages but felt that the children were nevertheless well taught. He said that spelling and composition could be better and that singing was rather lifeless. Good examination papers had been written by Trevor Lane, Nancy Willetts, Herbert Hambridge, Mary Pearman, Cyril Hambridge and Jim Turner. The inspector found that the lower group was very interesting and quite good answers were made by:

> Doris Willetts, George Tubb, Gerald Jeacock, Janet Winter, Eric Nicholls, Vera Smewin, Michael Wadsworth, Joyce Weston, Harold Herridge and Donald Steptoe.

> The Bishop's prize was awarded to Leslie Heredge and certificates were given to Trevor Lane and Nancy Willetts.

Success came to some children in May when 19 certificates and 38 badges were given out in the 'Clean Hands' campaign. In the same month Herbert Hambridge and Peggy Herridge received certificates for attendance and Jim Turner, Nancy Willetts, Trevor Lane, Roland Barguss, Leslie Heredge and Beryl Stimpson gained certificates for conduct and progress. There seemed to be a drive for better health and cleanliness amongst children as dental inspections were introduced about this time. Cleanliness of some of the children continued to be a problem for several years and in 1937 the head mistress wrote:

> It has been necessary to repeat my talks on the dirty state of the children. At times since my headship here I have found this a very trying matter and among many there is a general indifference to appearance.

May 24th 1933, Empire Day, was celebrated in style. A flag was hoisted in the playground and the children marched out and saluted. The infants recited and the older division performed a short play. After a talk, the National Anthem was sung, which concluded the Empire Day demonstration.

The harmonium in the infants was disposed of at about this time. The pipes were sold for 5/- and the wood was used for brackets and a wall table in the school.

In June an attempt was made to give children staying on the premises a chance to have a hot meal for 2d or 3d according to numbers. Only one child responded. The meal, which cost 3d, consisted of meat, potatoes, cabbage and rice pudding.

The HMI inspection for 1934 produced the following report:

> The number at this school which appears to have been fairly stable during recent years has of late shown a rather sharp increase. There are now 61 children taught by the head mistress, Miss Smith, and a supplementary assistant, but from the nature of the rooms the school is probably more comfortably worked by two teachers than it would be with a staff of three. The mistress who came here in November 1930 is hard working. She has no easy task with a class containing scholars of all ages from 7 to 13 years and varying greatly in ability. She has a most sensible way of managing the class, giving all the individual attention possible and doing her best to interest both the brighter and the duller children. She trains them all to work hard and to work quietly and appears to get the very best out of each of them. The teacher in the infant school works on similar lines and obtains similarly good results.

In December 1934 it was recommended by the Berkshire Education Committee that a senior school would be more suitable for children over the age of 11. The vicar suggested that they should attend Boxhill C. of E. School, in Abingdon.

In spring 1935, Leslie Heredge won a fountain pen in a painting competition and about the same time the children at the school collected 141 eggs for Abingdon Hospital. Many older members of the Women's Institute in the village will remember doing this for many years afterwards.

Beryl Stimpson won an OXO fountain pen in 1936. She was interviewed for this book and gave her reminiscences. She remembers her head teacher being short and plump with bright red hair and was rather scary. When Beryl first started school, she was taken on a bicycle by her mother who was on her way to work at Radley College. Later Beryl went with Steve Tubb and the Jeacocks. There were no organized games at that time but Beryl remembers playing hopscotch, skipping and ball games in the playground. The girls took part in tap dancing after school as an extra. Some children went home for lunch but like most of the children she took sandwiches to be eaten in school. Sometimes she had a hot drink at lunch time in winter with Mrs. James (Jean Merry's grandmother), who lived in the cottage opposite the church. Jeannie James was her friend at school along with Doris Willets and her sister. Beryl remembers lining up at the gates of the school if the funeral of an important person were taking place. In 1935 it was the Silver Jubilee of King George V. Everyone in the school dressed up, representing people from different countries of the Empire, and paraded up to Radley College. Beryl went as Cyprus.

Brian Talboys was at the school for a brief period between 1935 and 1937. He remembers Mrs. Smith, the head teacher, being very strict and someone with whom his mother often disagreed. Mrs. Smith used to take the children into her garden to cut the grass and Brian on one occasion was given a big and dangerous pair of shears. Other memories he has are of the birds nesting in the outside toilets, the school catching fire, resulting in it being closed for some time, and the daily milk being put by the large coke stove in the classroom and becoming warm and tasting unpleasant. The children drank milk through a straw. He remembers the iron framed desks with seats that folded up at the back, the slates and chalks and the exercise books for the senior children. The boys in those days had to do knitting and raffia work and he kept making mistakes but Doris Mattingley (now Willetts) helped him. He felt the standard of education at that time was very low. The vicar who visited the school was the Rev. Francis Daly Briscoe, who was the incumbent at Radley from 1936 to 1939.

The weather had not featured in the log books for some time. However, in June 1935, it was reported that a severe thunderstorm had begun shortly after 2.30 p.m. No-one could read or write. The infants were made to rest their heads on their hands on the desks and sleep whilst stories and talks were given to the whole school. The dividing doors were opened. It was a hot July and classes were often taken out of doors. While outside one day, two boys killed a grass snake.

Fire drill was instigated in October 1935 and the signal was two loud whistles and one long soft whistle. The older class cleared in a quiet and orderly manner and in less than a minute they were in their lines in the boys' yard.

Sixteen children left to go to Boxhill Church of England School in January 1936 and Radley became a Junior and Infant School. Fifty children remained on the register. In 1939, Mr. Harvey, the headmaster of Boxhill School, organized a meeting for local head teachers to try to obtain some uniformity amongst contributory schools. Mrs. Smith failed to mention in the log book whether this was achieved but the Abingdon comprehensive schools were still trying to put this into practice 60 years later.

The diocesan inspection referred to the problems that the school had experienced when the fire had broken out in the school in 1935 and wrote that, while a few children were below standard, most were satisfactory. The best papers were done by:

> Gerald Jeacock, Michael Wadsworth, Donald Mattingley, Harold Herridge, Christopher Wadsworth, Alan Jeacock, Sidney Hambridge, Beryl Stimpson, Margaret Harris, Joan Willetts and Betty Heredge. The Bishop's prize went to Gerald Jeacock and certificates were given to Margaret Harris and Donald Mattingley.

Beryl Stimpson (now Buckle) still has the New Testament prize she was given for religious knowledge.

In 1935 there is an entry in the log book stating that the medical officer for health was unable to approve the milk supplied by Mr. Drysdale, which he obtained from Mr. May. The milk supplier needed to obtain a grade A licence and then the situation would be reviewed. The following week the school received milk from the Co-op. In October 1938, 26 children received one third of a pint of milk per day and two children paid for more of it. Some children had milk in a different form very soon afterwards when an accident occurred as the children were entering the porch. Several children were covered with milk when the milk container fell off the shelf on to Michael Wadsworth. The timetable was altered to enable the teachers to wipe it off the children.

In the summer of 1936 there was a dispute with members of Radley Women's Institute. The head teacher sent the following letter to Mrs. Stevenson at Radley College:

> I understand from the children that some parents propose taking their children to the outing organised by the Women's Institute. I write in relation to school attendance in the possible event of some mothers desiring their children to accompany them. I understand from the attendance officer that a communication has been addressed to all WIs in regard to this matter by the education secretary. I would be grateful for your support in the matter.

Mrs. Stevenson replied, 'Will you kindly have posted to me the letter to which you refer'.

Mrs. Smith, the head teacher, wrote to the Education Secretary at Reading who had sent the letter, and she forwarded a copy to Mrs. Stevenson. The trip being organised was to Bognor Regis on July 21st and 14 out of 52 children on the school roll went with their mothers. Mrs. Stevenson said that the problem regarding the children being absent would not happen again.

At the end of 1938 a school savings scheme was introduced into the school. In the first week 5/- in 6d and 1d savings stamps was collected.

During 1937 and 1938 most log book entries consisted of matters relating to the children. One boy was playing cricket with a tennis ball and, while trying to catch it, hurt his foot on a tree stump. His concerned mother arrived at the school and the head teacher had to call in the school nurse to confirm that the foot was alright. Nevertheless, the boy had two days off school. Another mother called at the school to say that some boys had eaten her son's orange the day before. The boys were ordered to take in ½d each as compensation. A girl called Eugenie fell into the pond before afternoon school and had to have her clothes dried at a neighbouring cottage. Mary Shayler remembers that there was a wall around the pond; children used to like walking on it and invariably fell in. On one occasion a girl from a poor family fell in and when they dried her they found she had been sewn into her clothes for the winter. Brian Talboys remembers that the wall was falling in when he was at the school and the children spread rumours that a woman was buried underneath it. The police sergeant was called in to admonish a boy who was seen throwing a tennis ball at ducks on the pond. One girl was punished for terrorizing the other children and making her brother kick a newcomer to the school. Several children were stung by wasps and a blue-bag was applied.

From April 1938 the school became known as Radley Junior Mixed. Children were permitted to have up to one week's holiday with parents per year during term time.

In September there was a fair in the village for two nights. Many children were up until midnight because of it and some fell asleep at their lessons the next day. There continued to be problem children at the school and in November a girl took her Alsatian dog with her to school. This was the second time it had happened. Miss Smith sent her home with a note for her mother and received a threatening and impertinent verbal reply. The child then played in the road with the roadman and made no attempt to enter the school. However, in the afternoon the child's sister asked if she could return and the head teacher agreed.

The first mention of war came in September 1938 when Berkshire Education Committee informed the head teacher that there was a possibility of it happening. At the beginning of 1939 a visitor from the 'Office' (Berkshire County Council) called to ask the children to circulate the village with the news that gas masks should be taken out of their boxes and examined regularly.

On January 19th 1939, Miss Smith attended the funeral service of the 'squire's' eldest daughter, Catherine Eirene Dockar-Drysdale. The children stood in silence by the fence as the family carried the coffin to the cemetery. Prior to her ill health Kitty Dockar-Drysdale had taken a keen interest in the social activities of the children.

In April 1939 the names of the streets and the numbers of houses in Radley were reorganised by Abingdon Rural District Council, which meant that the addresses in the admission book against the children's names had to be altered.

At the end of April, after going for several interviews over preceding years and being absent for several periods owing to ill health, the head teacher, Agnes Smith, resigned. Mrs. Bevan became the temporary head teacher during May and June. During that time there was an inspection which said that progress in the infant school was steady but the efficiency in the upper division was at an extremely low ebb. It was difficult to find a subject about which any but the brightest children showed any knowledge. The children failed to show their customary good manners and their written work was meagre in untidy, neglected books.

Miss Cross became the head teacher in July 1939 and would remain at the school for the next 35 years.

Chapter 7

The People 1939 - 1974

Head Teacher

Miss Marie Rosina Cross - July 1939 - August 1974.

Assistant Teachers, including those who were part-time

Miss Middleton - October 1927 - August 1971.
Mrs. Shepherd - before May 1941 - January 1942.
Miss Gower - A trainee to begin with - September 1942 - January 1946
Mrs. Annie MacKay - November 1946 - December 1947.
Mrs. E. Hayes - February 1948 - August 1955.
Mr. T. Ray Osborne - April 1954 - August 1988.
Mrs. Ullmer (née Hughes) - September 1955 - August 1956.
Mrs. M. Ellis - September 1956 - December 1956.
Miss Beryl Lewis - January 1957 - August 1958.
Miss I. D. Adlam. - September 1958 - April 1959.
Mrs. Berrington.- April 1959 - August 1959.
Miss Courtenay - September 1960 - August 1964.
Mrs. V. Gardiner - September 1964 - December 1965.
Mr. Clarke - September 1966 - August 1968.
Miss D. Clapham - September 1966 - August 1968.
Miss I. Bisby - September 1968 - ?
Mrs. A. Scott - September 1968 - August 1969.
Miss J. Partridge (later Mrs. Beard) - September 1968 - April 1971.
Miss Susan Beech - September 1969 - ?
Mr. Howard Lee - September 1968 - August 1979.
Mrs. Carr - September 1971 - July 1988.
Miss W. Reynolds - September 1971 - August 1974.
Mrs. Margaret Pickavance - September 1973 - ?
Mrs. F. Stuart.(French) - November 1960 - August 1962.
Mrs. E. A. Snowden - September 1962 - August 1966.
Mrs. B. M. Hallum - September 1962 - ?
Mrs. Margaret Whittingham - September 1964 - August 1968.
Mrs. Lay - January 1966 - August 1966.
Mrs. Taylor - January 1966 - August 1966.
Mrs. Eyres - About September 1964 - August 1972.
Mrs. Mary Hutson - May 1965 - August 1973.

Mrs. Torrence (for French) - September 1969 - ?
Mrs. Valentine (for French)- September 1971 - ?

Supply Teachers

Mrs. Rita Steel.
Mrs. Baron, (Miss Middleton's sister).
Mrs. Shepherd.
Mrs. Cross (Junior).
Mrs. Mantell - (February 1942 to July 1942).
Mrs. A. E. Lock.
Mrs. Fuller.
Mrs. Bradley.
Mr. Bradley.
Mr. Bullock.
Mr. Lay.
Mrs. Rowson.
Mrs. Jackson.
Mrs. Sylvia Egelstaff.

Secretary

Mrs. Joan Poirette - January 1963 - 1976.

Caretakers

Mr. S. Ponting - 1946 - 1976
Mrs. Ponting - ? - 1976

Cook/Caterer

Mrs. Wilson.
Mrs. Blanche Cook.

Assistant Cook

Mrs. Godwin.

Dinner Controllers

Mrs. Brackley.
Mrs. Portsmouth.

On September 3rd 1939, Great Britain and France declared war on Germany. Two days later Miss Cross, the recently appointed head teacher of the school, was informed by Shire Hall at Reading that the school should be closed as it would be needed that day for evacuated children and all staff were to be present. No evacuees arrived as there were none in the village. Miss Cross reopened the school according to instructions received from the Education Secretary and had a gas-mask practice. Some parents said the children disliked wearing them but all put them on except for one child, who agreed after some persuasion. During October Helen Greening had work experience at the school prior to going to college. Her entry there was delayed because her college had not been made air-raid proof. She took PT with both groups and art with the junior boys. The school had wire netting fitted to the inside of the windows, and the church became the air raid shelter. A stirrup pump and first-aid box were later delivered. In June 1940 the school had some air-raid practices. The staff could take the children in from play to the church with gas masks, books and dinners, etc. in 2½ minutes. Every child had its own place in church and had instructions as to what to do in case of bombs dropping in the neighbourhood. The children practised going under the pews. Marjorie Whiting (née Wilson) remembers Colin Smewin had to drop a chair at the back of the church to give the effect of bombs dropping. She recalls that she was more scared of the spiders and mice in the church than the bombs. There were several air-raid alerts and the school went into the church each time. Once, the 'all clear' siren sounded at 4.30 p.m. The teachers kept the children in the church until their parents came to collect them and most of them had gone when the siren went. One mother arrived, shouting at the top of her voice, and was most abusive about the fact that the staff had kept her child there instead of sending him home. Miss Cross decided to refer the matter to the LEA. An officer went to see the mother who said at first that she was an atheist and was against her child going into a church, then admitted finally that she had been in a bad temper. On another occasion, when an alert went just as the children were leaving school, Miss Cross had to make the decision to send the children home quickly rather than take them to the church, which was cold and damp.

During Miss Cross' early years at the school, treatment of injured children was rather different from today. In October 1939, during playtime, a girl was hit on the head by a board which had been knocked over by her sister. Although the child appeared to be unhurt, Miss Cross took her into the school house and put her to bed until the end of afternoon school. On another occasion a girl knocked a desk top onto a boy's head. Miss Cross washed it with Dettol and cut away his hair. She took him to the Warren Hospital, where Dr. John Fisher instructed the nurse to stick the wound together with sticking plaster. Miss Cross then took the boy home. In the meanwhile his sister had been sent to tell their mother about the accident. Another time a child fell against the barbed wire and cut his leg and hand. Miss Cross this time used Jeyes Fluid to bathe the wound, then strapped it up with Elastoplast. There was a programme of immunisation for diphtheria being undertaken in 1941 and Radley children took part in it with the result that the disease gradually became eradicated.

On July 27th 1945 a girl came to school with something in her eye. As her eye failed to respond to washing, oil was put in by the head teacher and the girl was sent to the Warren hospital, in Radley Road, Abingdon. She was accompanied by another girl who knew the way. The outpatients department repeated the treatment and recommended that she should go to see Dr. Preston straight away. The children had to return for some more money and were sent to Abingdon on the 1.50 p.m. bus. As both children were frequently sent to Abingdon to shop, the head teacher decided to send them in, unaccompanied by an older person. In 1948 when a girl fell and cut her finger on the barbed wire, the wound was washed and she was sent home with a note to ask her mother to take her to the hospital or doctor. No antiseptic was used, which would enable the doctor to apply his own.

Mick Portsmouth started school at about the same time as Miss Cross became head mistress. He felt that she was strict and would give the cane when necessary, but if a child wanted to learn she would do all she could to help. He remembers doing all the main subjects but very little in the way of practical activities such as woodwork or cookery. There were no organized sports. He went home for lunch and took sandwiches for mid morning break. Milk was free for the children. One of his vivid recollections was of some of the school children walking into Abingdon in 1940 to see a German aircraft displayed in Roysse's Court. The pond was very different when he was at the school; it was surrounded by grass, as can be seen in the photograph later in the book. In better weather there were ducks on it. He remembers that the boys' offices were not covered by a roof and this wasn't very pleasant when the weather was inclement.

At the beginning of 1940 there was severely cold weather and there were problems with very cold classrooms and frozen pipes. Water was collected by the boys at playtime from the farm across the road. For the first time since war was declared a ton of coke was delivered for the stove, for which Miss Cross was most grateful. The need for conserving coal, used on the open fires, was made obvious when she had both classes in one room as she was worried that the open fire burned two buckets of coal each day. One day four infants were found playing on the pond at 3.45 p.m. Miss Cross kept them in school until 4.0 p.m. as it was not considered safe to be on the pond before 4.30 p.m. The ice was springy in the middle before the temperature dropped in the evening.

Eventually on February 5th the thaw set in. The school had been without water for three weeks. Many children were absent as was the cleaner through illness. Miss Cross' father lit the fires and the children kept the school clean and tidy. The vicar, the Rev. Eustace Edward Arthur Heriz-Smith, said that, if the cleaner were ill, it was the cleaner's responsibility to find a replacement and the substitute should be paid out of his wages.

By the end of February the playground was a sea of mud. The teachers, however, managed to organise a Red Cross skipping competition. The winners were:

Forward skipping	D. Ede (1020 skips). A. Jeacock. J. Herridge
Backward skipping	V. Turner
In pairs side by side	Margaret Saunders and Joan Hellman
In front	Elizabeth Hellman and Muriel Hadland

Six shillings were raised and at about the same time the children brought in pennies and raised the same amount for Finnish children.

Miss Cross dealt with children who were late for school by keeping them in for the equivalent time, especially children who were late because they played on their way to school. She caned children who had been fighting and throwing things and she caned a girl for constantly doing bad work. The girl had not tried to improve her examination books and her behaviour in school had been unsatisfactory. Miss Cross even smacked two children at their mother's request, for playing truant, as the mother had no influence over them at home. In October 1953, when a child injured another one by throwing a brick, the culprit had punishment 'in the proper place'.

The diocesan inspector in 1940 was impressed by the capable head teacher, who had made a splendid start. He thought she was teaching along sound lines.

A new approach to the infants' education came when they listened to a wireless lesson, sitting outside a window of Miss Cross' school house in order to do so. By 1948 they were able to listen to King George VI and Queen Elizabeth's silver wedding service of thanksgiving on the wireless in the classroom, but it was not until 1959 that they had a long-playing record player.

Miss Cross completed an interesting survey of parents' occupations in May 1940. Out of 35 children in the school only four parents worked in rural occupations, e.g., gardeners, woodmen or cowmen. All other parents, she wrote, worked for the GWR or at Morris Combine (a name given to the factory at Cowley) or followed other occupations in Abingdon or Oxford. It is likely that some fathers at this time would have been serving with the armed forces but others could have been in reserved occupations. In the parish records for the war years, about 20% of the fathers of children baptised were in one of the armed services. Most of these men were serving in the army but there were some serving in the RAF, the US Army and the Royal Canadian Air Force. In addition to these there were men and women who were not yet parents. Fifty-three men from the village are known to have served in the armed forces during the war. The war claimed the lives of at least six men from the village and changed the lives of many more. Amongst those who died was John George Thomas Smewin, who was killed at Dunkirk aged 19. He was the son of John Cyril and Elizabeth Mabel Smewin.

Lessons must have been rather different on the day when Mr. Greening, the farmer at Church Farm, Radley, gave Miss Cross a dead fox cub, which she showed to the children. On the same day Mr. Badcock brought in a live grass snake, which managed to escape down a hole under the floor. On another occasion the timetable was altered and the children listened to a wireless programme entitled 'If you were French'. About this time the boys finished the garden by the vicarage gate. The vicar gave Miss Cross a large quantity of stone, which she used to make a raised bed. These stones probably came from the demolished smithy, which once stood by the school, and were possibly used later for the churchyard wall.

The inspector, in his 1940 report, expressed his approval for the improvement in the junior department. He felt that attention should be given to reading and number work with the infants, where the children needed to concentrate more.

The school children were again having to carry gas masks in May 1940, following the invasion by the Germans of Holland and Belgium and attacks on French territory. The school holiday in May was extended because a large evacuation was expected. Mr. Campion and Dr. Agneau came to inspect the village hall in Lower Radley in case it was needed for medical examination in the event of an evacuation. In June, 34 evacuees arrived from Upper Hornsey Road School in Holloway, London, and made the village hall their schoolroom. Marjorie Wilson remembers their coming by train. It was agreed that six infants could come from the evacuee school in return for help from their staff with the older children at the village school. Four of these returned to the evacuee school soon afterwards as they had more staff there. Miss Cross commented that on June 27th there had been no air raid the night before, which resulted in the children not feeling tired the next day. While the evacuee children were using the village hall, Lily Hadland was caretaker there. She received 7/6 a week for a job which included cleaning, taking the bookings and unlocking and locking the hall before and after every use. More a labour of love than a job!

Gas mask drill took place one morning. The infants had to wear their masks for a quarter of an hour then rest for 30 minutes. Miss Cross ordered boxes for the gas masks and made it known to the authorities that a lot of the masks had the mica broken. They were still waiting for replacements many months later. The children had to learn how to put on each other's masks and also how to use the stirrup pump and approach a fire.

Miss Cross' ability for teaching bell ringing was first shown in April 1941, when the children gave a handbell-ringing concert in Abingdon for the War Weapons Week. During that evening they played for a social in Kennington. Miss Cross remained a bell ringer for most of her life and only retired from it in 1996. This was the same year that she was awarded an MBE. She felt that bell ringing was good because it reminded people about church and religion and she said that you can't shut bells out. The children continued to perform at concerts from time to time over the years that Miss Cross was at the school. One of the school's pupils, Pete Turner, used to pump the organ in church as there was no electricity supply to it. Jenny Ford (now Davie) became a bell ringer at the age of eight, standing on wooden fruit boxes to reach the ropes.

At this time the class numbers were as follows:

Miss Cross 24   Mrs. Shepherd 22   Miss Middleton 24

Miss Cross was very much in favour of taking the children on visits and these included one to Iffley to see the Norman church. The party travelled to Kennington by bus then walked the remaining distance. She also took them to Oxford to visit the cathedral (Norman work), New College (city wall) and the Botanical Gardens. Children of the two top classes went with Mrs. Shepherd and Miss Cross to a war-weapons exhibition in Abingdon, in accordance with the regulations of the Education Committee. Another time they went for a nature walk along Sugworth Lane, Radley. During one nature walk the children collected rose hips for the national collecting service. They collected 10 lbs. in half an hour. Another day they took a walk to see the weathering effect of a stream. In June 1942 the children went to Abingdon to see an educational film show at Boxhill School put on by Amey's, a local company. In May 1943 some of the older children with the vicar, the Rev. John Vincent Pixell, and Miss Cross cycled to Woodstock after the service for Ascension Day. Some years later, in 1958, she took a party of children to the London Science Museum and London Zoo.

In July 1941 the boys, during their spare time, cut thistles in the meadow next to the playground and then put them into ricks. Their usual playing field was very dry and the grass was dying, whereas the rest of the field was covered with long grass and thistles. The boys worked for Mr. Greening, the farmer, who was very short of staff, in return for the use of the field during playtime and lessons. In May 1942, during the last quarter of an hour of the school day, the boys raked up straw which had blown all over the place in the high winds. The playground was where the tarmacked area between the old school and the newer building is now. The children also played on the field, which is now the new cemetery.

The diocesan inspector reported, on August 1st 1941, that:

> In Class II the teacher's lesson was presented in a way which obviously interested the children and held their attention throughout. The children could answer questions very well on work previously done. In Class I the teacher had lost her voice but the children answered the inspector better than the previous time. Their written work, though, is below average for children of this age group. Some children found difficulty in expressing their ideas in writing. The successful attempt to link the parish church and school more closely is to be commended.

In December 1941 about 72 children started to have school dinners. This number included the evacuee children. On the first day the dinners arrived at 1.45 p.m. and were finished by 2.30 p.m. The clearing up took roughly half an hour. The next day the dinners arrived at noon and the children were ready for the afternoon session of school on time. In January 1942, during a very cold spell of weather, the dinners were cold when they arrived and there was not enough stew. The children were allowed to slide on the pond instead of having PT that day, which perhaps compensated them a little for the poor meal. By the 19th January 1942 the roads were frozen and like glass, the stove went out during the night, the caretaker was ill and there were deep drifts of snow. Only 16 children managed to arrive at school. Miss Cross had to make an OXO soup and a milk pudding as there were no school dinners. When the meals were not delivered the next day, Miss Cross sent the children home for their meal. On February 2nd Miss Cross went to see the head of the evacuee school to find out why 50 dinners were ordered and only 34 were served. Using the left-over food she decided to heat up the vegetables and gravy the next day and sell them to 'go into the school dinner money'. On March 24th the meat for the school dinner had gone off. Several children and staff were sick in the afternoon. The head teacher wrote a letter of complaint to the catering manager at Reading. The same month she received a licence to sell food and went into Abingdon to procure a milk permit for 66 one third of a pint milk bottles per day. On another day the dinner-van driver forgot to leave the potatoes. Mrs. Gowring, who lived near the school, phoned the Abingdon garage, which her husband owned, to try to stop the van but was not successful. In December 1942, the rice pudding and potatoes were covered in rust from the lids of the bins. A complaint was sent to the catering officer at Wantage.

On April 14th 1942 Miss Cross admitted 11 infants. The junior children in the larger room had to sit at trestle tables, which were also used for dinner, as there was not enough furniture in there for them. There were then 77 children on roll. Miss Cross had to borrow ten bottles of milk from the evacuee school. While there she found out that it would be closing at the end of the month and any remaining children would have to go to her school.

In May 1942 the drill lesson was interrupted by aeroplanes flying overhead. Some extra chairs and tables were found and brought to the school.

Infantile paralysis (polio) appeared in the village in July 1942 when several boys at Radley College suffered from it and were put into quarantine. Any children who had been in contact with the college boys also had to go into quarantine for 14 days. Sixteen years later, at the beginning of 1958, Salk vaccines were given to the children at the school to prevent them from catching this dreadful disease. In the same year as the polio outbreak occurred in the village there was an outbreak of foot and mouth disease among cattle. Mr. Greening asked that the children should not play in the meadow for six weeks. To give the children more room in the playground, Miss Cross organised play into two shifts.

In August 1942 Mrs. Mantell, the regular supply teacher, left the area as her husband had been moved to a different station. The managers could not find a replacement for her, which meant that one of the older girls helped Miss Middleton with 'the babies'. On September 28th Miss E. J. Gower arrived at the school, having been sent by the local labour exchange. As she was due to be called up for government service, she said that she was willing to try teaching if she could be trained. After an interview with the vicar and head teacher it was decided that Miss Gower should have a month's trial to see if she could do the work. This agreement was ratified by Berkshire Education Committee when the vicar telephoned them. It was extremely difficult, if not impossible, to get supply teachers and one day, when Miss Gower and Miss Middleton were absent, Miss Cross had to run the school on her own with the help of the older children.

As the number on roll went up to 81 in November 1942, Miss Cross realised that there was not enough room in the school to hold a medical inspection. She wrote in the log book that it had been decided that Mr. Hutchin's house at 78 Foxborough Road would be used, as the LEA were still paying for it. The boys had to take the necessary furniture down.

At the end of November it was impossible to read in school as it was a foggy and dark day. Miss Cross fetched a gallon of oil, which would be for the lamps that were used, there being no electricity in school until a couple of years later. In December 1942 the children put on a concert and £2 was raised for the Red Cross China Fund and the Waifs and Strays Society.

There was a diocesan inspection in January 1943 and Radley was considered to be a splendid school. The children were keen and interested and made good responses. The inspector said that real credit was due to the teachers.

In May 1943 a 'Wings for Victory' week was held. A concert and dance took place in the village and nearly every child went to it, which meant the children were quarrelling and very tired the next day. Consequently half an hour of rest had to be given in the afternoon.
W. O. Fairman of the R.A.F. came to the school and addressed the children on 'Wings for Victory'. He told the children about bombers and answered their questions. Thirty of the older children went with Miss Cross to an exhibition and films in Abingdon.

When the older children transferred to Boxhill School in Abingdon, they were each issued with a bicycle in order to get there. In June 1943 Mr. Davey, the attendance officer, called at the school to say that if any bicycles hadn't arrived by the date when the children should transfer and a child had no other form of conveyance, then the child should stay at the village school until the bikes had arrived. June Weston's bicycle was not delivered before July 31st, which was the end of the school year but not the end of the summer term. She had the bicycle in time for September. From July 1945 all children moving on to secondary school started there after the summer holidays.

114

The end of 1943 saw Miss Cross going to a conference on fuel economy and the children giving another concert in aid of the Waifs and Strays Society. That term the children worked on a survey of the village and the traffic using it during their geography lessons. Tests of children's ability in the main subjects were regularly carried out.

'Salute the Soldier week' took place in June 1944. There was a visit, at 3.0 p.m. on June 23rd, from Mr. White, the deputy mayor of Oxford, and Councillor Edgar Alfred Smewin, the sheriff of Oxford. Mr. Watkins, the chairman of the local national savings committee, was also a VIP. They were met by the vicar and one of the managers. The vicar introduced the visitors to the children. Mr. White then spoke to them, followed by Councillor Smewin, who had been a pupil at the school. The head mistress proposed a vote of thanks and three cheers. The Mayor and Mayoress of Oxford also paid a visit to the school later in the evening for a school concert. Eleven pounds was raised and this was invested in savings certificates for the school building fund. Ninety-six children were then on roll.

Mr. Buston of the Ministry of Supply came one afternoon in July to talk to the junior children on the necessity for a greater drive on the book recovery campaign. On the morning of July 25th the Abingdon RDC van called to collect books for the 'Books for Forces' drive. About 1000 books had been collected by the school. George Steptoe collected 250 books and became a 'Field Marshall' and Geoffrey Hellman a 'General'.

By September 1944, during the dinner hour, the boys were collecting wood for the fires from Mr. Shaw's sawmill, in Lower Radley, but by January 1945 he was not able to let them have any more. Fortunately the bursar at Radley College had two large piles of wood which needed clearing in a hurry. The children managed to do it in two lunch hours and one afternoon.

Miss Cross had to measure the children's feet to find out if they were long enough to qualify for extra vouchers as practically everything which could be bought was rationed by this time. Seven girls were eligible. This happened again the following year. In the years after the war, chocolate powder was distributed to the children to take home about twice a year.

The state of the school in January 1945 was summed up in the inspector's report. It said:

> This is a 3-class school in which the two youngest classes of 30 and 25 respectively share a dismal room which is overcrowded and difficult to keep clean and tidy. These circumstances do not allow the teachers to give the children the fundamental training which is the school's function. The children have also suffered from the absence of staff which has sometimes left the head mistress entirely responsible for over 80 pupils.

115

The limited facilities for other suitable activities lead to a concentration on the '3 Rs' with the younger groups. The method of teaching reading was discussed with the teachers and certain modifications on present practices were suggested.

In the top class the present age range is from 7 to 11 years. The atmosphere in this room is somewhat restless due in part to unavoidable interruptions. Because the head mistress must attend to matters apart from teaching, it would be well to provide a certain amount of carefully graded individual work as a basis for habitual training for these children. The class showed itself interested in oral work and was of average ability in English and arithmetic. Pupils would achieve better results however if more were expected of them throughout the school. Nor should it be difficult for the teachers to stimulate the children to greater and more continuous effort for one of the pleasantest characteristics of the school is the prevailing spirit of cooperation.

It was hoped that one class could occupy an annexe room at the vicarage but Eastbourne College, which had been evacuated to Radley, was using it. The infant class eventually moved there in October 1945.

Charlie Steptoe was at the school between 1942 -1948 and he remembers two teachers, Miss Cross, who was fair but strict, and Miss Middleton, who was tall and slim and played the piano. He remembers there was one big coke stove in the old building and that it could be very cold in there. The school dinners came in big churns and were left at the school gates. Everyone had school meals and he felt they were good except for tapioca, which they called 'frog spawn'. There were, however, some children who disliked the meals. Brian Ford was at the school a few years after this and his recollection of school dinners was that he liked them but agreed with Charlie Steptoe about the 'frog spawn'. The Rev. Pixell was the vicar and he came into school on Friday morning each week. Nearly all children belonged to the Sunday school and Brian Ford still has his Sunday school stamp book, which recorded his attendance. Recreation included sliding on the pond in winter and getting to school early to collect the walnuts off the tree in Miss Cross' garden, as well as playing with a tennis ball on the playground. On one occasion Brian won a prize for writing.

1944 saw the introduction of the Butler Education Act, which established the tripartite system of secondary schools, i.e., grammar, technical and modern. It defined the modern split between primary and secondary education with the introduction of the 11-plus examination.

January 1945 was cold and snowy. The thaw set in at the end of the month but the dinner vans could not get through as the roads were impassable. Where possible children were sent home for lunch. Those whose parents were out at work had hot cocoa, toast, bread and jam in school. One day 20 out of 84 children were present. Miss Middleton and Miss Cross were

116

able to do the stock-taking while Miss Gower taught them all. The school had to close for one day because the playground was too muddy and this prevented the children from going to the offices.

When the county scholarship exam was taken in March of each year, the remainder of the school had to go out on a nature walk or sit in the church to leave space in school for the 11+ children who were taking the examination. In 1945 children not taking the examination went to Big Wood camp. This was where the evacuated units were until July 24th 1945, when the camp was no longer needed. The equipment and supplies plus the remaining nine children were transferred from Big Wood to Radley School.

During the afternoon of May 7th, news came that the German wireless had announced the complete surrender of all German forces on land, sea and air. The head teacher told the children to listen to the wireless that night and, if May 8th were declared VE (Victory in Europe) day, which it was, there would be a holiday for two days.

October 19th 1945 was a special day for the school children and Miss Cross' family. They were invited to the baptism of the head teacher's niece at 3.45 p.m. in Radley Church. About 50 children attended the service, which was taken by Rev. A. G. G. Thurlow, Precentor of Norwich Cathedral, for the baptism of Jane Elizabeth Cross, daughter of Lieutenant Commander Robert Gordon Cross RN and Irene Stella Cross of Hove.

In January 1946 Miss Gower informed the school that she would not be able to continue teaching owing to the ill health of her mother. Mrs. Bradley came as a supply teacher for a while but obtained a permanent post in Oxford. Mr. Bradley came for odd days. Later in the month Mr. Bullock started at the school. He was not qualified but Miss Cross agreed to retain control of the class for a month while he took groups. During the following year he took exams in order to qualify as a teacher. He went with children on visits to look at the newly built houses in Radley, which the children were studying. He also took some children by bus to the Ashmolean Museum and the Natural History Museum in Oxford and for dental inspections in Kennington. He left for a permanent post at Warborough School, in Oxfordshire, at the end of 1946. Mrs. MacKay took his place as certificated assistant.

There was quite a lot of sickness in the village in the spring term of 1946. Many children had mumps and chicken pox and there was a nasty germ going around the village which caused upset stomachs. Miss Cross wrote in the log book that it was 'not green apples' causing it. Wounds from falls, etc. were washed with iodine administered by an older pupil.

In September 1946 there was free milk for all children. It was often freezing cold in the winter and unpleasantly warm in summer.

1946 was the year when Anne Blundell (née Picton) started at the school. She then lived in Foxborough Road but later moved to Radley Road. It was from there that she either cycled to school or went by bus. She remembers that Miss Cross, Miss Middleton and Mrs. Hayes were her teachers. Miss Middleton's classroom was in the vicarage and the children used to walk round to there with tiny blackboards under their arms. The room used was in a building near where the church room is now. Jenny Davie, at the school about the same time, remembers Miss Middleton as a calm, gentle person who never seemed to change over the years. Mrs. Hayes was a very strict teacher and not very popular because of this. She used a ruler to admonish the boys and was known as Tabby Hayes. The main subjects taught at this time were maths, English, art, geography, RE and history. Miss Middleton taught sewing and knitting. Anne and Jenny learnt to play the recorder while they were at the school and took part in school assemblies, which were taken by the vicar every Friday. PE was held on the small playground outside the old building. Every Friday Miss Cross' class emptied the flowers from the church and washed the vases, etc. Mrs. Hayes left the school in 1955 to become a head teacher in Devon. Before she left Miss Cross presented her with a flower bowl, a book about castles and a book token. She spoke with gratitude about all the work Mrs. Hayes had done behind the scenes, such as doubling up her class in order that other teachers could go to the music and dance festivals and about her excellent work with less able children, especially in helping them to learn to read.

The notoriously bad winter of 1947 caused many problems for the school. There were 77 children on roll, Miss Cross having admitted seven children belonging to 'show people' who lived in 'The Pit'. According to Rita Ford, who was born and brought up in the village, this was where Catharine Close now stands. On the 29th January there was a very heavy fall of snow. Only 36 children were present. The temperature in the classroom was below 40 degrees Fahrenheit at the start of the school day. The temperature in both the schoolrooms never went above 40 degrees Fahrenheit all day except near the fires, and the heat from those could not be felt two yards away from them. It remained like this for several days. The vicarage room, which was warmer, was used instead of the large classroom but no written work could be done as the desks in there were too small. The children wore their coats but continued to feel cold. The thaw set in about February 3rd but the bad weather returned and more snow fell. This continued into March and on March 5th Miss Cross reported deep snow and drifts. Twenty-eight children were present and they only had enough coke to last for three days with no possibility of replacing the supply. The head teacher lit the fires as the caretaker could not get through the snow. No buses were running, which meant that Miss Middleton and Mrs. MacKay had to travel by train. No school dinners were delivered on some days owing to the bad road conditions, which resulted in the children having to walk home for their a midday meal. On March 6th only 12 children attended school. As three teachers were present they were able to teach four children each. On 13th March there were no dinners as the van and the relief van were stranded in 4 ft. of water at Hanney, south west of Abingdon. By the 18th March the cottages in Lower Radley were cut off by the floods due to Sandford Lock breaking under the pressure of water flowing downstream. The night before, there had been a great gale which enabled the children to go out 'wooding'. March 19th was a very dark, wet day and the school could not take advantage of the electric lights because of a ban on the use of electricity. There was no coke for the stove and only about a month's supply of coal, which they could only use in the small grate in the large room. The plate heater was not being used because of electricity cuts and the copper could only be heated at 12 o'clock.

The weather gradually improved and on May 13th forty-eight children accompanied by staff, parents and friends set off for Whipsnade Zoo. The weather was fine and warm and it was a very successful trip. Abingdon Coaches transported them and the cost was approximately 4/- per child.

In June 1947 Princess Elizabeth visited Radley College as part of its centenary celebrations. There was a firework display in the evening and many children stayed up until 1.30 a.m. to watch it, which resulted in their being tired the next day. Miss Cross represented the village school at the garden party. The Warden invited the children to watch Field Marshal Montgomery arrive at the college on 17th June to review the junior training corps as part of the centenary celebrations. Monty leaned out of his car and said 'Good morning' to the children who were lining the drive. The children watched the inspection from the archway and later wrote a letter of thanks to the Warden.

In September 1947 Miss Cross radically changed her method of teaching. She decided to do far more activity work throughout the school. This meant a much more fluid timetable was kept and the children were not inside the school building as much as they had previously been. Class III undertook a survey of Church Farm and the part of the village near the church. Class II surveyed the school, the playground and the field. It meant that formal English, history, nature study and geography disappeared from the timetable and syllabus. Miss Cross decided to keep formal arithmetic with some modification. Reading with the infants was silent reading and to a certain extent cropped up as the children required information on certain subjects. Art and handicraft were closely allied to the child's own activities. Needlework, however, had to be kept as the girls were acquiring skills for their secondary schools. The inspectors were soon there to see what she was doing. Miss Murton, HMI, Mr. Crawford, HMI, and Mr. Gillett, the Assistant Director of Education for Berkshire, visited the school on November 10th. They invited Miss Cross to take as much work as possible to Reading on November 22nd for discussion about it. She had in the meanwhile received a letter from the Director of Education to say that she could continue with this type of syllabus. Following this new method, Class III went to see Mr. Taylor's dung spreaders working at Sugworth Lane and also to the Ashmolean Museum in Oxford to see Radley's Iron Age finds. Some children visited White's plantation, on the college side of White's Lane, Radley. Class III measured various Upper Radley buildings for their model.

In February 1948 Class III visited the station as part of their activity work and Miss Rabley, HMI, accompanied them. Miss Rabley was obviously all in favour of this new method of teaching as she called to collect some of the children's work for a conference in a neighbouring county. The work Miss Cross was doing continued to be used by inspectors for some time afterwards and some of it went to the Festival of Britain on the South Bank, in London, in 1951. Miss Cross and 14 children visited the exhibition. Jenny Davie (née Ford) remembers that on a visit to Radley Church the children were able to make brass rubbings, learn about its history and look at the stained glass windows, etc. They studied nature and knew the names of flowers and trees. They also enjoyed pond dipping.

The children were given a day's holiday for the royal wedding of Princess Elizabeth and Prince Philip on November 20th 1947 and several years later for the wedding of Princess Margaret on May 6th 1960. Queen Elizabeth II made a visit to Abingdon in November 1956 and the school children went to see her on that occasion.

During 1948 the school cleaner was often ill. The replacement lady offered to do the job at 1/6 per hour. This rate went up to 2 shillings the following year, which was the standard rate for women in the village.

In February 1948 the children organised a jumble sale, which raised some money to buy books for the library. On the following Saturday six girls went into Oxford to buy six books with the money they raised.

During the summer of 1948 Miss Cross arranged for the 24 junior children to go swimming at Hinksey Pools, Oxford. Anne Picton and Jenny Ford remember going soon after Easter, whatever the weather. There was a district sports day in June.

57 children were on roll in September 1948. There had been several cases of offences against young children in the area and during this month three children had to attend the assizes in Reading as witnesses.

In November Nurse Sullivan attended the school and, according to Miss Cross, it had a 'clean sheet' for the first time on record.

There was a shortage of milk in September 1949 as a result of the drought. The assistant supervisor of school meals called round about this time to talk about equipment for the new canteen being built. When the school took possession of the new building in February 1950, the dining room section was used by the infant class, which had moved out of the vicarage. Prayers and assembly were also taken in the new building as it was more satisfactory than the cramped conditions of the old one. Dinners actually started to be cooked on the premises in September 1950. Anne Picton described the dinners cooked by Mrs. Wilson as 'wonderful'. By 1959 Miss Cross was writing that it was difficult to get people to work in the kitchen as locally there was a large demand for labour.

Radley School with the pond in the foreground. Date unknown but thought to be about 1950.

From about November 1949 students at Culham Teacher Training College undertook teaching practices at the school. In later years students from Westminster College, Oxford, which later merged with Oxford Brookes University, were there.

There were occasional visits from the local police. In March 1950 they called regarding housebreaking and the destruction of property known as Church Cottages. The head teacher was asked to enquire into the matter as it was felt that local children were involved. This proved to be the case and many children were guilty of trespassing on the property. Those who had done the damage owned up to it. In October of the same year Constable Horne came for a school report with regard to 'two old boys' who had been accused of stealing a sack of corn. Later he warned boys about their behaviour in the village when he came to ask people not to pin notices on Mr. Greening's barn door. A year later the vicar, the Rev. J. V. Pixell, who was at Radley from 1941 to 1957, was warning boys that they would be caught if they stole any more eggs from people in the village.

There was a carol service in the church in December 1950. Miss Middleton played the organ for it and some of the Radley College boys rang the bells before the service started. The church fortunately was warmed up before the singing started as it was a cold day.

121

In January 1951 Miss Cross went to St. Edmunds R C School to show them how to use the film strip projector. She seems to have been very interested in visual aids and was on the committee to choose films. She was also very involved with organising the folk dance festival held in the Abbey grounds, Abingdon, each summer. Anne Picton remembers her mother making a black, gypsy-type skirt for her to wear at this event. In the same year the school became a controlled school under the provisions of the Education Act 1944, and from then on the powers of the church authorities in the day-to-day running of the school became limited.

From about 1950 Miss Cross started admitting children with special needs. She admitted four boys from Dr. Barnardo's orphanage in Abingdon as all the schools there were full. She also accepted several children at the request of the child guidance clinic in Abingdon. In October 1953 she wrote that she had admitted 10 children since the term began, from schools all over the country, and only one child could read well, one could read below average for his or her age but the rest could not read. There was one child about this time who tended to run away and Brian Ford vividly remembers both Miss Cross and the child rolling on the floor on several occasions when she tried to stop him. Brian also has memories of the school dentist coming to the school in a caravan. It put him off dentists for life as Brian describes the visit to the school dentist as 'horrific'. It had the same effect on many children.

In February 1952, Class II children walked into Abingdon to hear the proclamation of Queen Elizabeth II. Twenty-four children from this class went to Portsmouth in May. In June 1953 they went to the cinema in Abingdon to see the film 'Elizabeth is Queen'. The children were allowed to watch the coronation on a tiny TV set in Miss Cross' house. A coronation committee was set up in Radley and the school received £7, which together with the £17 they had collected went towards a wireless unit. Many people in the village contributed. The wireless set cost about £17 and two speakers were bought for two classrooms costing £5 each. The staff paid for the fittings and two friends of the school installed the whole set. The LEA gave a grant towards the final cost of £45 and paid for its maintenance. There was also a gramophone turntable attached to it. The July 1953 *Parish Magazine* listed all the donors and the amount they gave.

At Christmas in 1953, following what could have been a disastrous arson attack on the church, the children held their carol service. All the tree decorations had been destroyed in the fire but the children brought in gifts in kind or money to pay for new ones and the tree looked very presentable. The choir was issued with new cassocks, surplices and hymn books. The Rev. Pixell was at Sunningwell Church with Radley schoolboys Brian Ford, Bruce Gaskell, David Herridge and Peter King, when the news of the fire reached him. There then followed a hair-raising dash by car to Radley by the vicar, who was not known for his careful driving. The boys accompanying him were terrified.

By May 1954 there were 114 on roll and there was a great need for extra accommodation. The village hall in Lower Radley was available and was used for four half-days per week. At first each class went for half a day per week, but later Class IV stayed at the school and Class II, who could use it more profitably, went for a whole day. Many children were coming in from the Woodland caravan site on the northern fringe of the parish and by April 1955 the school was larger than ever with 127 on roll. Consequently everyone was delighted in September 1955 when surveyors were seen pegging out the land for the new school buildings.

Mr. Osborne had joined the staff in April 1954. He came from an Abingdon secondary school where he was the PE teacher. Preferring to teach younger children, he retrained and obtained the position of assistant teacher at Radley where he found Miss Cross to be somewhat formidable and rather frightening to many children and parents, but nevertheless someone who was very much in charge of her school. He worked well with her and respected her but thought it was interesting that she always called him Mr. Osborne whereas other teachers were called by their Christian names. He thought that Miss Cross' organizational skills were first class and she always had her fingers on the pulse. If anyone needed help or advice, she was always there to give it. He recalled that at one time she was asked to work at Oxford University's education department teaching foreign students who were often head teachers and deputies.

During summer 1954 the school competed against other small local schools,- Wootton, Appleton, Kingston, Longworth and Sunningwell- in a junior sports competition. The following children were successful:

30 yards, boys aged under 7	Paul Gaskell 2nd
40 yards, aged 7 - 8	Boys - Richard Tabor 2[nd.]
	Girls - Judith Gill 3[rd.]
60 yards, girls 9 - 10	Lesley Robinson 1st
70 yards, aged 10 - 11	Boys - Richard Brackley 3rd
	Girls - Jean Allen 3rd
High jump, aged under 10	Boys - Michael King 1st - 3' 2"
	Girls - Lesley Robinson 1st - 3' 4"
High jump, aged over 10	Michael Hornblow 2nd - 3' 10"
Long jump, boys open	John Wilson 1st

Radley was unable to take its turn in hosting the sports day as it had no playing field at that time. Despite this, the Radley team managed to win the shield for the highest number of points won by one school in both the 1955 and 1956 events. Mr. Osborne's skills as a PE teacher paid dividends for the school when they competed against other schools. He coached the children and success followed success, which caused a little resentment with the other local schools. In the end, after winning the shield for four years in a row, he agreed that, to try to make it fairer, the other schools could choose which of Radley's two teams his competitors would go into. Radley then came first <u>and</u> second.

Radley Primary School Athletic Team, 1957

Winners of Area Schools Shield

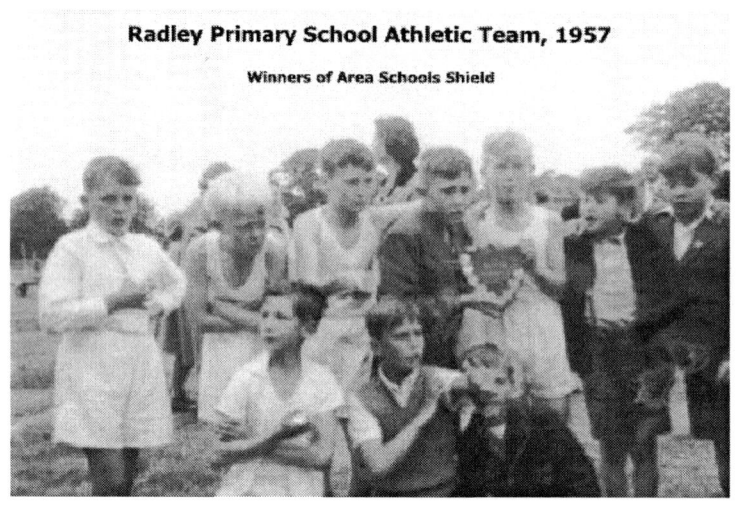

In December 1954 Rita Wilson (now Ford) was congratulated on receiving a bronze medal for swimming. The vicar thought that she was the first girl from Radley to obtain this.

Miss Cross wrote an article for the *Parish Magazine* in February 1955 and said:

> At a recent inspection of bicycles by WPC Trotman the bicycles of the following children were passed as being satisfactory: V. Kyme, J. Cottee, C. Smewin, M. King, A. Purbrick, A. Dunsden, C. Cato, L. Robinson, P. White, K. Mattingley, J. Gill and B. Tubb. It is hoped to hold another inspection later this term and that then a larger number of children will have bicycles, which can be passed as satisfactory. I should like to point out to parents the necessity for seeing that all bicycles have two adequate brakes and that saddles are the correct height.

In July 1955, parents were invited to watch dancing and PT displays in the school grounds with a PT tableau by the children, staged by Mr. Osborne, to conclude. There were displays of craft work produced by the children and Miss Middleton accompanied, on the piano, the choir and recorder players. This was the summer in which Mrs. Hayes left and Mrs. Ullmer, who had previously been teaching in London, took her place.

Earlier in the year the children in Class IV collected 10/- towards the fund set up by the vicar of Bray to restore his church. The children had been learning the song, `The Vicar of Bray` and made a collection when they knew the church there needed £5000 to restore it.

In January 1956 Miss Cross decided to make great changes in the teaching of the infants. She wrote:

> As both Classes I and II consist of children under seven it has been decided to make every afternoon a `free activity` afternoon. Miss Middleton and Mrs. Ullmer will take charge of groups of activities and not of their own class as such. It has been felt for some time that Class II needed more freedom and it will give Mrs. Ullmer some experience of this type of work and of working with infants.

In the *Parish Magazine* Miss Cross thanked many parents for giving gifts of toys, puzzles, dolls, books, cookery sets, doll`s furniture, tea sets, etc. to the school. These were probably related to the new type of teaching, which she was introducing. Two pairs of boxing gloves were given to the school later in the year. A local person gave some spades to enable the boys to dig out a jumping pit. Mr. Osborne supervised the digging and made some of the apparatus to be used with it.

Eighteen children, accompanied by Miss Cross and Miss Middleton, visited the Whitechapel bell foundry in London in June 1956 to see where the new treble bell for the church had been cast. They were able to see one of the new Bow bells being tuned and saw the moulds for the Great Bell of Bow, which was to be cast the following week. They also visited the Tower of London, had a trip on the river from Greenwich, climbed the Monument and saw other famous sites. Miss Cross congratulated the parents on how well turned out their children were and how nice they looked in their new school uniform. She hoped that the following term all children would wear the uniform of plaid skirts and blouses for the girls and grey flannels for the boys. Striped dresses could be worn by the girls in summer. Mrs. Ullmer left the school at the end of this term as she had not been well. Mrs. Ellis agreed to teach for one term until a replacement could be found.

About the middle of September 1957 the new school buildings were finally opened. They consisted of two new classrooms and a new cloakroom block. The two classes in the canteen were able to move into these new classrooms and the canteen was used as a dining room and a practical room. The number on roll was 116 with many of the children being caravan dwellers. At this time parents were having to pay £4 . 5 . 0 per week for the rent of a caravan. In January 1958 a child was admitted to the school whose age was not known but she was believed to be about six. As far as could be ascertained she had never been to school before. Her parents had gone away leaving her on Shaw`s caravan site, in Lower Radley, to the care of anyone who would look after her. To begin with Mr. and Mrs. Shaw cared for her, as her parents could not be traced, then two officers from the Children's Society called to collect her.

Mary Shayler's daughter Ann Thorpe attended the school from 1954 to 1961 and she kindly gave an interview about her time there. She was a pupil at the school when the old buildings were still being used and the two new classrooms and toilets were built. There was the separate canteen as well. They had no playing field, just an over-grown meadow and a sandpit for long jump and high jump. The school continued to have two-seater desks but some classes had roller blackboards. The subjects she studied were English, arithmetic, history, geography and nature study. The children worked on projects and Ann was given one called 'sandpits'. She visited Tuckwell's gravel pits, at Thrupp in Radley, and was shown a mammoth tusk. Miss Cross took the children on nature walks but one turned out to be rather unfortunate for her. They were out on a walk through a farm where pigs were kept when she slipped in the mud and became very dirty. Ann remembers that the children were taken to Hinksey Pools, in Oxford, for swimming lessons and it was very cold. She had lunches cooked at the school and remembers having to sit at the table until everything was finished. Games, which they played in the playground, included, conkers, jacks and marbles. On Brownie 'Thinking Day' the girls wore their Brownie uniforms.

Linda Thomas was a pupil at the school from 1957 to 1963 and remembers the fine italic handwriting which was taught by Mr. Osborne. The school became quite well known for it and secondary school teachers recognized Radley children as a result. Children in Classes 1 and 2 used pencils but Classes 3 and 4 used pens and ink. Linda also remembers the school dinners cooked by Mrs. Blanche Cook. There was a special mash of potato and swede. Puddings included jam tart and apple tart served with custard. At that time the Rev. Robert Springett Brutton was the vicar and he visited the school once a week. He was a popular vicar who tried to welcome everyone to the village and encourage them to partake in village activities. Often he could be seen walking home with the children and visiting their families. Linda remembers that during thunderstorms, if the children were outside, Miss Cross made them take off their spectacles and any other metal items in case of lightning.

In September 1957, Miss Cross received information regarding the exclusion of children who had been in contact with Asian 'flu. The next week she commented that they were fortunate in being the only school holding their own with the 'flu. The following week, however, they had to close. When the school reopened, she admitted the 13th child since the beginning of term who could not read.

Radley Football Club was using the land at the back of the school but Miss Cross had to send a warning letter to them in October 1957 saying that the field they used had only just had the crop cut and they were responsible for the insurance if anything happened to any children or to the school building. They could use the field until it again went under the plough and then it would be rested for two years. After that it would only be used by children attending the school. It was levelled and grassed in 1959.

In 1958, out of 136 children on roll, 40 of them lived in caravans. Housing was still in short supply after the war and this was the only home some people were able to have. In July 1958 there appeared to be some clearing out of Shaw's caravan site. The Rural District Council had set up a committee of enquiry into caravan sites as all of them had more than the licensed number of pitches. At this time the caravan sites in Radley brought to the neighbourhood a fluctuating population and to the school a number of children who were 'birds of passage'. Ninety-five children were admitted from caravan sites between January 1954 and 1958, of whom 46 left without completing their primary school courses. They had entered the school, at various ages, from around fifty different schools and, since many of them had disjointed school careers, they came with varying standards of attainment. Mr. Osborne thought that the school roll was greater than 200 at one time. Classes of about 36 children were the norm.

There was an inspection by HMI in June 1958 and the following is the report:

> Enlightened schemes of work arising from a cultured concept of primary education have been prepared by the head mistress. Now she has a larger staff to guide, she would be well advised to add a general preface in aims and methods. The timetable is well arranged having regard to the special aptitudes and abilities of the staff and to difficulties due to lack of space in the old building. Greater use might perhaps be made of the dining room. Some of the needlework and craft periods are rather long.
>
> The entrants' class is taken by an unqualified teacher who combines formal class teaching with some of the activities associated with an attractive and well-equipped infants' room. By a blending of these two methods the children are given an introduction to the basic skills before passing to the second class, which is in charge of a progressively young teacher who uses her artistic ability to full advantage. The room is attractively arranged and embellished with varied samples of the children's work in art and craft. Plenty of reading material is available. A number of children read with fluency and enjoyment and achieve good standards of computation and handwriting. Exceptionally good illustrated free expression work takes place not only in the small booklets based on scripture, history and geography topics but also in large folders on group topics and in story writing.
>
> That the traditions of cooperation, interest and industry inherent in the head mistress' scheme for education are accepted by late entrants to the school is not

only a tribute to the firm establishment of these traditions but is also the keynote to the sound and lively work in the upper part of the school. The challenge presented by the admission at this stage of some backward and retard children in need of remedial teaching is readily accepted and the methods employed meet with commendable success. This side of the work is carried on without curtailment of the interesting local studies and topical work which have long been an outstanding feature of the work of the school.

While the new classrooms were being built, a very full study was made of the plans and of the materials and processes involved. The children readily turn for information to the carefully chosen and well-used collections of reference books. Some very good free writing occurs based on all subjects of the curriculum. Standards of presentation are good.

In arithmetic the two classes are regrouped on ability. Though somewhat dominated by text books, the work is reasonably accurate and well set out. The master has recently embarked on a course of elementary science carried out under great difficulties because of lack of facilities for practical work. An interesting variety of work takes place in needlework and craft lessons. The school day begins with an assembly in which the children take a full part. Until recently, the school provided a church choir and a recorder group to accompany some of the services. The head mistress, who is a keen bell ringer, is also able to provide the ringers. Boys and girls are skilled in flower arranging. The school regularly competes in music and dance festivals, sports and athletics meetings and swimming tests. During each year there are educational visits to London, Oxford and Abingdon. The school meal is cooked on the premises and well conducted on a family basis in the dining room.

This is a good school in which the children are interested, friendly and working to capacity. That the school has survived and surmounted so many difficulties without lasting detriment must be due to the inspiration, resilience and powers of leadership of the head mistress.

In September 1960 Miss Cross wrote in the log book that:

Class IV and III girls walked to Sunningwell as part of the tests they were doing to develop initiative and leadership, etc. Mr. Burton called today to discuss a tie-up with a London school who are studying the upper River Thames. They will spend a fortnight at Big Wood holiday camp in July and Radley will pay one visit to the London school.

The new climbing apparatus is now in position and use. The children have raised £10 for it by collecting paper. They are now collecting paper to pay for a picture they want.

The children from Netley School in London arrived in April 1961 and the Radley children accompanied them on their visits. Miss Cross felt it was fruitful for all concerned. When not out on visits, the London children worked in the village school alongside its usual pupils. Radley children visited the London school for one day and managed to add in a visit to the Tower of London.

There were 120 children on roll at the beginning of the 1961 autumn term but several families who had lived in caravans for six to eight years were moved to houses in Oxford. This meant that the roll dropped to 95. It stood at 108 in May 1962 with 31% of the children from families who lived in caravans. In September 1962 the Rural District Council opened the caravan site at Pebble Hill, on the northern fringe of Radley, which meant an increase in children once again. During the previous six years, the school had admitted 206 children and of those 117 remained. There had been a turnover of about 50%. In November of that year 48 out of 120 children lived in caravans. In 1963, 54 children travelled by bus to and from the Oxford direction each day. Miss Cross applied for a warden to escort the children to the bus after school but in January 1967 she was still told it was unlikely. In 1966 she removed the infants' afternoon break to enable them to catch the bus at 3.20 p.m. This meant that 36 children went on the first bus and 30 on the second.

The school started French lessons in 1960 for the better children with a part-time teacher, Mrs. Stuart, who was a French specialist but French teaching was spasmodic. In later years other teachers on a very part-time basis were brought in to teach the language. Mr. Hill was giving swimming lessons in Radley College open air pool in 1962 and Mrs. Snowden and Mrs. Hallum started as remedial teachers. For the first time Miss Cross could have some secretarial help from January 1963 when Mrs. Joan Poirette was appointed to do the job.

1963 was another notoriously severe winter. In January there was snow and ice from the beginning of the year and the attendance was very poor. Some parts of the village were cut off, particularly Peachcroft to the west. There were 5 and 8 feet snow drifts between the school and the council houses in Church Road but the snow-plough and man-power kept the road open. There were deep drifts outside Park Farm, Radley, which resulted in single file traffic. Miss Cross was pleased that Radley School had managed to keep all the pipes unfrozen even though a number of schools had to close because of burst pipes or boilers or lack of fuel. At one point the school was down to its last day's supply of coke but more arrived. The diesel fuel in lorries was freezing, which caused problems with the transport system. At the end of January, Radley School also suffered from frozen pipes in the outside cloakroom for the canteen and Class III's cloakroom. The River Thames was frozen over and the caravans at Pebble Hill were without water as many pipes were frozen. There was a brief thaw at the end of the month but then people had to cope with leaking pipes. Snow fell again at the beginning of February but it was not as heavy. The weather remained cold but it was not freezing during the day.

Miss Cross seldom wrote about having to punish a child but about this time she had one very troublesome child. She wrote that she had to slap the child on ' the place made by nature for reception of same'.

A new classroom, hall, staff room, head teacher's room, library space and entrance space were added to the school in 1963 and Miss Middleton's class moved into the new room. The hall was used for assemblies but Miss Cross found the acoustics unsatisfactory. Class IV moved into Miss Middleton's old room and felt lost after their previously cramped conditions in the old building. The small room was then used for craft lessons.

At the beginning of January 1964 the children from the new St. James' Road estate started at the school. There were some worries over the 'bus children' getting to and from school and the parents tried organising a private minibus but this would have cost 1/- per day per child, which was too expensive. In April Miss Cross had sabbatical leave to study maths teaching in the USA.

In January 1965, with 138 on roll and following a measles epidemic, Miss Cross introduced ITA (Initial Teaching Alphabet) as a pilot project. ITA was devised by Sir James Pitman, grandson of the man who invented Pitman's Shorthand. It used the normal 26 letters of the alphabet but also 14 other characters to represent sounds such as 'oo' and 'th'. Its aim was to provide a logical spelling system. The theory was that, as children became fluent in ITA, they would become more aware of conventional spelling and move then to the normal alphabet but it was not always successful. Parents generally were not happy with the ITA system and voiced their opposition to members of staff. During April 1975, Mr. Stephens, Miss Cross' successor, delivered several boxes of ITA material to St. John Fisher's school in Oxford. Rumour has it that Radley School was the last school in the country to use ITA but perhaps that record might be held by the Oxford school. Mrs. Sharples, who joined the school at the same time as Mr. Stephens, had to learn how to use this system at the beginning of her teaching career, just before it was phased out.

An example of ITA.
Translation = The ice angel gave the owl a ring.

130

In June 1965 Miss Cross was able to be a non-teaching head as she had 157 on roll by then.

On the night of February 16th 1967 thieves broke into the kitchen, picked up a 7lb weight and smashed their way into the head teacher's office, where the filing cabinet was broken into, completely ruined and £11 stolen. The CID was called and fingerprints taken.

In May 1967 the county's civil defence officer visited regarding the possible use of the school as a rest centre in the event of a major disaster in the locality.

1968 saw many local education committees cutting back on spending. Radley was informed that because of the economic state of the country they would have the same capitation grant as the previous year. This virtually meant a 25% cut as already many things had gone up 33.3%. Schools could not employ a supply teacher until a member of staff had been away ill for one week. This took effect where a non-teaching head was responsible for a school. There would also be a cut in the employment of part-time staff. Changes were made at the end of term. Mr. Clarke left the school as the increase in petrol etc., due to the budget, had put his travelling expenses out of all bounds (30 miles a day and petrol 5s.7d per gallon!). He had found a job three miles from home. Mrs. Whittingham obtained a permanent position at St. Nicolas' School, in Abingdon.

In June 1968 Mr. Osborne, Miss Dale and Miss Williams with nine Class A children set off to stay at Rhoose YMCA training centre near Cardiff and had an enjoyable eight days there.

Always ready for new initiatives, Miss Cross encouraged Miss Partridge, one of the teachers, to attend a course at the North Berkshire College, in Abingdon, on the 'Integrated Day'. This became a feature of Oxfordshire/ Berkshire Schools and in later years visitors from abroad came to see how it worked. In September 1968 she decided to ask Mrs. Carpenter and Mrs. Talboys to visit the school on a regular basis in order to talk and play with some difficult children. This proved to be very worthwhile.

There remained a very transient population of school children in 1969. Some of these children needed extra care and attention. Miss Cross wrote:

> Regularly six children are at school before I open the doors at 8.20 a.m. For a number of children school is the place for them where they are really looked after. This is an important part of the work of the staff. Since September 1967 we have admitted 67 children and already 16 have moved on. Between September 1966 and September 1967 we admitted 49 children and of these 24 have left. 91 children in and out and we are supposed to be a village school!

131

The vicar at this time was the Rev. Sydney Ernest Allso who was in Radley from 1966 to 1971.

At the end of 1969 the teaching staff were on strike for more pay and at the end of 1970 there were power cuts as a result of the electricians' national work to rule. The lack of electricity caused disruption in the children's education, especially on dark days.

There was an influenza epidemic in the first half of 1970 followed by mumps. During this year the children visited local farms, the Cotswold Wild Life Park and Norfolk.

In September 1970 Miss Cross became a tutor at the Oxford University Department of Education for two days per week. About this time she was beginning to realise that parents could play a valuable role in the school and wrote in the log book that she hoped they would be involved, by doing various jobs such as repairing damaged books.

A 'Times Educational Supplement' reporter, Miss Frances Hill, came to the school on January 19th 1971 to interview Mr. and Mrs. Ponting on the work of a rural caretaker and to take photographs of them. The article was printed in February and included a description of the school, which included the statement that the building was partly constructed of Tudor bricks. It went on to say:

> Mr. Sidney Ponting has been the school's part-time cleaner-in-charge since 1946. Until last year he combined his job with full-time employment as a railway engineer, coming to school at four o'clock after his day's work, to put in four hour's cleaning. He has now retired from British Rail, after 42 year's service, and spends more time at the school, cleaning and lighting the stoves in the old building before the children arrive in the morning, and doing odd jobs during the day, as well as his evening work. Some years ago his wife joined the school staff as an assistant. She does the lighter cleaning, looking after the classrooms in the extensions, while he copes with the old building, and the new area's much-travelled passage and hall.
>
> Radley School boasts little in the way of new cleaning equipment. There is an electric polisher but Mr. Ponting is scathing about its usefulness considering it more of a liability than an asset. His wife says a vacuum cleaner is what is really needed. The Pontings do most of their cleaning with brooms and long mops. Mr. Ponting jealousy guards his newest broom from the teaching staff, tying it to a hook in the broom cupboard with a serious of ingenious knots he hopes no one else can unravel. This is necessary, he explains, because it takes only a month for a broom to become tatty and caked with dirt and he is issued with only four brooms per year. Mr. Ponting is regretful that he cannot keep the school floors highly polished, but to do so he would have to work all night every night.

He remarks resignedly that the school looks beautiful at the beginning of term, until five minutes after the children have arrived.

Of the three forms of heating in the school - wood burning stoves in the old building, central heating and storage heaters in the extensions - Mr. Ponting is responsible only for the first. He chops firewood during the day, to supplement the school's issue. For years he campaigned for a ceiling to be built below the tall vaulted roof of the original building, to keep in the stove's warmth, and eventually last year, his wish was granted. The roof began to collapse and it was decided that the work of repair should include putting in the ceiling he wanted. As a result, Mr. Ponting now needs to light only one stove instead of two in all but the coldest weather.

One occasion on which he remembers a lot of hard work was wasted was when a water pipe burst the day before the beginning of term and the workmen who mended it left piles of clay and dirt all over the newly scrubbed and polished floors. He laboured till half past ten that evening to clear up the mess. 'If anyone hadn't been used to it, they would have cried', he says, but he accepts such incidents as among the inevitable hazards of being a school caretaker.

Miss Middleton retired in July 1971 after many years of dedicated service to the school.

Miss Middleton's retirement presentation in 1971.

During the summer of 1971 there were problems with the local bus company. It started charging full fare for children travelling before 9.30 a.m., which resulted in their being late for school. Miss Cross eventually negotiated a season ticket rate with the company but this was not satisfactory and some families continued to send their children in at a later time. In November the bus company changed its schedule again and the children were then arriving 45 minutes late and having to wait 25 minutes for buses at night. The times of the school day were changed to accommodate this.

Measles inoculations were given by Dr. Harcourt Norris, the school doctor, in May 1972. There were then 157 children on roll. Miss Cross wrote in November that there was an epidemic of head infestation and scabies and that a large number of children had mutations of measles and chicken pox, etc. Whooping cough was starting. In February 1973, with 162 on roll, there again appeared to be a measles, chicken pox and German measles epidemic.

On 1st April 1974, under the provisions of the Local Government Act 1972, Radley, along with Abingdon and many other Berkshire towns and parishes, became part of Oxfordshire. From that date the Oxfordshire County Council and its education committee took over responsibility for Radley School. It appeared to have had little impact in the school as the log books indicated that life went on as usual.

In 1974 the school was permitted to admit the 'rising fives'. The number of children on roll had risen to 173.

Miss Cross retired in July 1974. At her request, arrangements were made between Mr. Greening (farmer), Radley College and the managers that the pond next to the school should be handed over to the care of the school for the use of the children. The only condition was that it should be fenced off from the remainder of the field.

Chapter 8

The People 1974 - 1993

Head Teachers

Mr. Roger Martin Stephens - September 1974 - August 1993.
Mr. Richard Pengilby - January 1987 - April 1987 while Mr. Stephens was on secondment.

Assistant Teachers including Part-time Teachers

Mrs. Carr - September 1971 - August 1988.
Mrs. Margaret Pickavance - September 1973 - August 1975.
Miss Joan Field (Mrs. Sharples) - September 1974 - August 1982.
Mrs. Carol Corner - About 1974 - August 1975.
Mrs. Jill Evans - September 1975 - About 1977.
Miss Linda Cardiff - September 1975 - About 1977.
Miss Sandra Gregory - September 1988 - April 1989.
Mr. David J. Stemp - January 1989 - August 1994.
Miss Ruth Lilley - April 1989 - August 1991.
Mrs. Christine Chambers - September 1991 - August 1994.
Mr. Nick Hawes - About September 1991 - December 1997.
Mrs. Collins - Sept 1975 - July 1976.
Mrs. Thomas - September 1976 - July 1980.
Mrs. Tina Lawrence - October 1982 - November 1982.
Mrs. Marilyn A. Smith - November 1982 - ?
Mrs. Julia Eaton - October 1983 - July 1985.
Mrs. G. Knight - September 1985 - December 1985.
Mrs. C. Lennie - January 1985 - ?
Mrs. Howells - March 1986 - ?
Mrs. Holloway - September 1986 - December 1987.
Mrs. J. Capel-Davies. January 1988 - ?
Mrs. K. Lock.
Mrs. S. Kirtley.

Supply Teachers

Mrs. Ward.
Mrs. Dot Hewlett.

Classroom Assistant

Mrs. Daphne Green - 1970 - 1992.

Secretary

Mrs. Helen E. Beckett - 1976 - 1988
Mrs. Lyn V Bailey.
Mrs. Pam Kinnaird - ? - April 1995.

Cook and Assistant Cooks

Mrs. Blanche Cook.
Mrs. Saczak - ? - December 1993.
Mrs. Crabbe.
Mrs. J. Mattingley.
Mrs. J. Beckingham.
Mrs. Allen.

Lunch time Controllers

Mrs. Richardson -? - 1976.
Mrs. P. Whittington.
Mrs. J. Hamp.
Mrs. J. Beckingham.
Mrs. Simpson.

Cleaner-in-charge

Mrs. B. Lacey - 1978 - 1995.

Cleaner

Mrs. P. Webb - 1976 - 1997.

School Crossing Patrol Person

Mr. George Steptoe - 1977 - 1979.
Mr. George Goddard - 1981 - 1990.
Mrs. Jay -1990 - ?

In September 1974 Mr. Roger Stephens became headmaster of the school. Before this he had worked in St. Nicolas' School, in Abingdon, and as deputy head teacher at Wolvercote School in Oxford. He kindly agreed to be interviewed by Radley History Club about his time as headmaster and said that his first impression of the school, when he took over, was of a very traditional establishment.

Following the scrapping of the ITA scheme for reading, Mr. Stephens and his staff had to find out what new schemes were available and how a new one could be afforded. It was hard work but eventually new reading books were obtained. One of the things Mr. Stephens is most proud of from his time at Radley is the fact that only one child was unable to read when he left the school and that was for a very good reason. A special needs advisory support teacher called Mrs. Wheeler visited the school on a regular basis and she was able to spend time with children who needed help. She took in support materials to assist them.

Mr. Stephens was keen to promote a closer liaison with the parents and one of his first tasks was to start a Parent Teacher Association (PTA) with David Beckett as its first chairman. The name of this group of people changed over the years and has at times also been referred to as the Parents Association, the School Association and the Radley Primary School Association. Parents were given timed interviews to discuss their children's progress and many of them came into school to help the staff. Mr. Osborne welcomed the fact that parents, with the encouragement of Mr. Stephens, went into his class to help with subjects such as needlework.

At the beginning of 1975 the school 'fayre' organised by the PTA raised £164 and in the same year the summer fete raised £160. As a result of this, the field was drained. David Beckett recalled that he, as chairman of the PTA, was told, at his first request to the LEA for drainage to be done, that the school would have to wait for about 13 years. However, he persuaded the LEA to pay half the cost if the school's parents could raise the other half, which they were able to do. Mr. Osborne remembers the grassy area, which became the playing field, being flooded quite frequently with little tufts of grass showing above the water. Before drainage it could only be used for about two months of the year.

Mr. Stephens worked hard to improve the interior of the building. One of the teachers, Mr. Howard Lee, and he tried to make the classroom in the old building a more amenable place. Carpets were laid in the library area and walls were fitted with hessian-covered pin board.

The children continued to attend the church for one service a week and the Rev. Daniel Legh Pope, who was vicar of Radley from 1971 to 1988, would visit the school as well.

For several years there was a caravan on the school premises, which was used by the staff for teaching small groups of children and later as a storage facility. David Beckett, when he was a governor, was able to negotiate a good deal with Mr. Deane, a local farmer, over the sale and delivery of the caravan and when it arrived, Mr. Bone, the father of a child at the school, helped to adapt it for use in school. The caravan was broken up and taken away in May 1994 as gales had damaged it beyond repair. The school's insurance policy paid for a new wooden building.

From June 1976 the children from the Woodlands caravan park were entitled to attend Kennington school. Although most caravan sites were on the edge of Kennington and within walking distance of the school there, they came within Radley Parish's boundary, which meant that children from this area traditionally attended Radley School. Siblings continued to be enrolled at Radley school but most children, from this point onwards, went to Kennington School. Children from the Peachcroft Farm Estate, in Abingdon but on the western fringe of Radley, were permitted to attend Radley School if their parents wanted them to go to a Church of England school or a village school. Some sections of the Peachcroft Estate were originally in Radley but were moved into Abingdon when the boundary was changed.

In July 1976 Mrs. Richardson (dinner controller) and Mr. Ponting (caretaker) were forced to retire because of a new ruling on age. Mrs. Lacey was given the post of caretaker. Mrs. Joan Poirette also retired at this time and Mrs. Helen Beckett became the school secretary, holding the position for 12 years until the end of 1988, when Mrs. Lyn Bailey took over. Later Mrs. Kinnaird, the vicar's wife, became secretary and she left in April 1995. The new secretary was then Judi Woodbridge. Mr. Stephens said he was very lucky to have had such excellent secretaries.

The numbers of children in school gradually reduced and by September 1976 the classes were as follows:

Mrs. Carr - 21
Miss Field - 25
Miss Cardiff - 22
Mr. Lee - 24
Mrs. Evans - 21
Mr. Osborne - 24

In 1976 trees provided by the CPRE (Council for the Protection of Rural England) were planted by the school children at the gravel pits near Pumney Farm. Four trees were planted in the school pond area and six trees along the south fence to the playing field. During the Christmas break some parents and staff enclosed the pond with a fence. Mr. Stephens was particularly interested in natural history and conservation work and one of the ash trees by the school pond came from his mother's garden as a sapling.

138

Difficult decisions had to be made about redeploying staff in March 1977. Eventually Mrs. Evans left on maternity leave and Miss Cardiff gained promotion by going to a school in Kidlington. The fate of Mrs. Thomas, as a part-time teacher, was also in the balance but her contract was renewed.

Miss Joan Field, who married and became Mrs. Sharples, was at the school between 1974 and 1982. She is now living in Cheshire but has very fond memories of the school. For the first two terms she taught the third class, then for about seven years she taught the second class and finally she taught on a part-time basis for about a year. Her teaching began in the smaller half of the old building, in a very poorly equipped classroom with very little space. There were only about 23 children in her class but she does not think any more would have fitted in. The classroom had a cloakroom attached, the blackboard was on the chimney breast and there was a storage heater in front of it which gave out heat at night but was cold in the daytime. She remembers leaving a tin of wax crayons on it overnight, which congealed into a nasty mess by morning. On another occasion the green wax crayons mysteriously disappeared. When they found green mice droppings, they discovered what had happened to them. Mrs. Sharples remembers that the teachers had to make most of their own equipment, e.g., work-cards, and there was no set curriculum. She introduced a new maths scheme which was made up of a 100 packets of cards. Children progressed through the packets at their own rate. The children wrote diaries and stories and learnt spellings for Friday's spelling test. A great favourite at that time was the television programme 'Watch', which they looked at every Tuesday morning. The large television had to be pushed into the classroom during morning playtime. This was a good programme, which stimulated other curriculum work. During the time Mrs. Sharples was in the school the parish council decided to erect some playground equipment by the new village hall, in Gooseacre, off Foxborough Road. Mrs. Sharples took her class down to see what was there as they had been asked to do some designs of what they would like. They then went back to school and drew their ideas, which they gave to Mr. Alan Clark, who was at that time chairman of the parish council. One of the clear memories Mrs. Sharples has of the school was of the good meals which were served and the lovely atmosphere at lunch time, when good manners were reinforced. She had close links with the church and restarted the Sunday school with Mrs. Liz Turner. Her marriage was conducted in the church by the Rev. Dan Pope and Rev. Jock Fletcher-Campbell, who were close friends of hers. The children were fascinated with her married name as it was the same as Ena Sharples, a character in the TV programme 'Coronation Street' at the time.

During the first few years of Mr. Stephens' time as head teacher, the school was broken into several times. Usually a window and/or a filing cabinet were broken and small items and petty cash stolen. On one occasion the thieves only stole two apples from the kitchen. There were some more serious thefts in following years. On one occasion in 1994 many items were broken or stolen.

In 1978 the spare room was carpeted for a television, projector and all-purpose room. There were then four classes in the school with the number of pupils as follows:

Mrs. Carr - 24
Miss Field - 21
Mr. Lee - 35
Mr. Osborne - 34

About 1979 a *Handbook of Information for Parents*, was produced. In it Mr. Stephens set out the aims of the school, which read as follows:

To explain adequately the aims of any school would require a whole volume. Briefly we aim to:

- Provide each child with as great a knowledge of the basic language and mathematical skills - the 3 R's - that the child is capable of, using tried and proven methods.
- Instil a knowledge of our culture and our world (history, geography, science, nature study and domestic crafts, music and art in its various forms) and to develop the children's physical awareness and abilities (PE and games).
- Teach children the skills of finding out for themselves.
- Teach the values of our Christian society and to get on and work with others in a balanced and disciplined way.

Mr. Stephens went on to explain in the *Handbook* that it was not the school's policy to routinely set homework but reading at home was always encouraged. Teachers gave lists of spellings to the children to learn at home and occasionally set finding-out tasks. There was no compulsory uniform but the following list was given as a very optional guide.

Girls.   White blouse, blue tie (when they can do it up themselves), blue jumper or cardigan, grey or blue skirt, white tights or socks. Blue and white stripes, check or spots for summer dress.

Boys.   White or grey shirt, blue tie (when they can do it up themselves), blue jumper, grey trousers, grey socks.

Winter.   (For grannies to knit), blue and white striped scarf, gloves and hat.

The *Handbook* presumed that mothers would be the parents who took the children to and from school and it referred to having parent-teacher consultations in the evening in order that fathers would not have to miss work.

In December 1979 Mr. Steptoe, the 'lollipop' man, retired after doing the job for two years. Mrs. Jay became the 'lollipop' lady or school-crossing control person.

More staff cuts took place in June 1979 and Mr. Lee accepted redeployment to Kennington School.

Mr. Stephens became a teaching headmaster in September 1979. The classes with their number of pupils were then:

> Mrs. Carr - Infants. - 18
> Mrs. Sharples - Upper Infants - 28
> Mr. Stephens - Lower Juniors - 30
> Mr. Osborne - Upper Juniors - 28
> Mrs. Thomas - Remedial groups and relief.

Louise Beaumont (née James) attended the school between about 1978 and 1985 and she remembers Mrs. Carr being a very caring teacher who always wore a lovely perfume. Mrs. Carr used to play the piano and behind it there was a box of dressing-up clothes. The children studied the normal curriculum but also had play activities. Louise's teacher in Year 2 was Mrs. Sharples and lessons were far more structured. Mr. Stephens was her teacher in Years 3 and 4 in the old building and Mr. Osborne taught her in Years 5 and 6 in what she described as a building rather like an air-raid shelter (the canteen). They had the original, old, wooden desks, which were carved with the names of past pupils. These double desks were in school when Mick Portsmouth was a pupil and he remembers the carved names on them. Louise particularly remembers Fridays when Mr. Osborne would give the children quick-fire questions. The reward for a correct answer was an extra hot mint. There was no photo copier and any duplication was done with a machine which needed a very carefully prepared master sheet and a strong smelling liquid. Her memories include the Rev. Jock Fletcher-Campbell taking services for the children in church each Thursday morning, very good school meals except for the cabbage, which was awful, and that, if you failed to eat the main course then you could not have the delicious pudding.

The prediction for pupil numbers for September 1980 was 87 and in July Mrs. Thomas was made redundant and Mrs. Sharples had reduced hours because of the falling roll. There seemed to be a gradual demographic decline in the school population of Radley. People were having fewer children and houses were not changing hands as frequently as they had before.

It was about this time that Alison Grimes and Ros Murdoch, her friend, were pupils. They are among the people who kindly agreed to be interviewed about their time at the school. Their memories are similar to other people's but they also mentioned the stage in the hall, which was used for nativity plays. It was built in 1980 by a group of parents. Alison and Ros remember the monkey bars, the dome climbing frame and the goal posts on the playing field, as well as the climbing equipment for PE in the hall. They recalled the stews, salads, faggots, shepherd's pie, vegetables, iced buns, semolina, blancmange, biscuits and green milkshakes, which 'tasted how washing up liquid smells'. At the beginning of 1982 school dinners cost 52p.

School milk ceased to be provided for children in April 1981. From December of that year the school had a governing body. Two parent governors were elected.

In July 1982, Mr. Stephens wrote, 'The school has been working towards raising 50% towards a micro-computer, encouraged by Mr. J. Perfect, chairman of the PTA, of Radley College, himself a computer expert'. That year the Parents Association made a big effort to raise money at the May 'Fayre', when Mary Bowerman was the May queen. As a result of a sponsored walk at Radley College over £350 was raised. Only three people walked further than the headmaster, who walked 13 miles. The computer arrived and an evening was arranged at the beginning of 1983 to show it to parents. Mr. Osborne and Mrs. Carr went on a computer course to learn how to use it. Mr. Perfect used to bring his Research Machines (RM) 380Z over from the College to the caravan and show groups of children what it would do. The county's IT department decided that it would equip Oxfordshire schools with RM computers rather than, at that time, the more popular BBC computers. The advisor for IT in the county had previously worked for RM, an Oxford-based company, and was very good at producing suitable software for the machines.

Mr. Stephens and a group of people interested in computers joined together to write programs which they sold to raise money for the school and fill a gap in the market in for middle junior children. The group discontinued their work when more sophisticated personal computers (PCs) arrived in schools.

In September 1982 the school was down to three classes. The teachers were:

Mrs. Carr - 24 pupils
Mr. Stephens - 33 pupils
Mr. Osborne - 30 pupils
Mrs. Evans 0.5 of a week and Mrs. Lock 0.2 of a week

During the 1982 summer holidays Mrs. Sharples had a baby and resigned. Mrs. Tina Lawrence took her job for a short time, then was replaced by Mrs. Marilyn Smith.

At the end of the year Dr. Jenkins said that she would no longer be going into the school as the school doctor. In future the health of children would be the responsibility of their parents or guardians.

In July 1983 Mr. Stephens wrote that it had been a successful year and that the school was becoming more balanced academically. For the first time in three years Mr. Stephens was not a full-time teaching head. Mrs. Julia Eaton was employed to teach for 0.7 days per week and shared a class with him.

January 26th 1984 was an important day when a disc drive arrived for the computer. Previously a cassette recorder had been used to install programs. It often took up to a quarter of an hour to load some programs and, if the beginning of the tape were missed accidentally, then the process had to be started all over again. Mr. Stephens attended a month's course at Westminster College, Oxford, in spring 1986 entitled ' The friendly micro'.

The same month the classes were given names:

    1 Foxborough
    2 St. James
    3 Stonhouse
    4 Bowyers

The children were very excited to watch chickens and ducklings hatch in March 1986, when Mr. Stephens borrowed an incubator from the county supplies department and Mr. John Homewood, of Peachcroft Farm, lent them an infra-red lamp to rear the newly hatched chicks. Mr. Johnson, the father of one of the children, stayed in school one night in order to care for the newly-hatched ducklings.

Parents had an important fund-raising role through the Radley Primary School Association and they formed a 120 club, which brought in a regular income. During 1986 they tried to raise funds for new games equipment and books for the library as well as supporting the classes. Parents also helped with transporting children on trips, at swimming lessons and supervising computer sessions. A few gallant workers cleared and improved the pond area with the intention of making it into a nature observation area. During the summer the School Association held a 'fayre' with a grand draw, where the first prize was a portable black and white television with Mrs. Kramer being the lucky winner. £239 was raised at the 'fayre' for School Association funds. Mr. Stephens remarked in the *Radley News* that the situation was so different from when he started teaching, when parents were not allowed past the white line painted at the gate, except for fund-raising activities and a termly consultation with teachers.

Children at this time were swimming regularly at the new Radley College pool, with the younger children swimming at Bennett House School, now the Kingfisher School, in Abingdon.

In 1988 the School Association bought a VHS video player/recorder for the school to enable it to make better use of television broadcasts. The usual car boot sales, jumble sales, 120 club and June 'Fayre' continued to be used to raise funds.

A week before a fun day at the school in May 1988, children of the top class joined with children from Dry Sandford to have an enjoyable educational and residential visit to Scarborough, Yorkshire.

In August 1988 Mr. Osborne took early retirement in order to do other things than teach. In his interview he said that his work at Radley had been enjoyable despite the ups and downs which come with teaching. He only remembers one major inspection of the school, which lasted about a week, but inspectors called in to school occasionally and were there to give advice when asked for. There were strong links with the church and at the start of his time at the school the children repeated the catechism. Teachers made up their own syllabuses and he liked the freedom to do this. He felt that children learnt better if the lesson plan wasn't rigidly followed. He often prepared work then was diverted by something one of the children said and the lesson would go along a very different track. Nevertheless the children had learnt something they were interested in. He went on several educational visits which included Hill End near Farmoor, Norfolk, Cogges Farm Museum in Witney, the local cement works and South Wales, which was an area he knew well. His aim in retirement was to play more golf and he was still doing that the day after his interview in 2007.

As the 6th Log Book was concluded in February 1989, Mr. Stephens wrote, 'The 1988 Education Act brings too much too quickly'. The Act introduced the National Curriculum, which made it compulsory for schools to teach certain subjects and syllabuses. Standard Assessment Tests (SATs) had to be taken by the children at various key stages. These were at ages 7 and 11 for primary schools. League tables were introduced showing performance statistics together with formula funding, which meant that more money was available to schools who had more pupils. Parents could (in theory) choose which school they wanted their child to go to. Schools, if they wished to opt out of local government control, could become grant-maintained schools.

By the end of 1989 Mr. Stephens was writing that the term had been very hard for pupils and teachers alike. The requirements of the national curriculum training required teachers to be away from their classes more than was usual in any term, with the result that the children's education had been unstable, to a certain extent, because of the numerous supply teachers. Added to this the teachers had to get to grips with self-evaluation and also cope with a malicious flu bug that was around at that time. There was general agreement amongst the staff that SATs were bringing too much work for the teachers. In his recorded interview Mr. Stephens said that formula funding and parental choice brought problems for the school as other schools in the area were competing for children in order to boost their finances. A school in Abingdon at that time had a very good reputation and took about the equivalent of one class from Radley. This all changed several years later as it became once again the norm to send children to their local village school. In fact, in 2007, children from out of the catchment area were having to be turned away from Radley School as there was not enough room for them.

In March 1989 a contractor working on the roof asked for a 999 call as he had discovered a fire in the roof space where he had been felting. The fire brigade attended, but the fire was out. The children were not evacuated from the building but were prepared to leave if necessary.

Twenty-eight children from the school, with Mrs. Lennie and her husband, Mr. Stephens and Mr. Clive Rickett, embarked on a PGL Adventure Centre weekend at Worminghall near Wheatley in May 1989. Activities there included abseiling, Canadian canoeing, mini motor-bike riding, orienteering, archery, fencing and rifle shooting. It was thoroughly enjoyed by all who went. PGL was founded by Peter Gordon Lawrence and he is one of the originators of summer camps for children. The initials became known as "Parents Get Lost", but that no longer applies as the company now operate a programme of family holidays.

The successful visit of the previous year encouraged the staff to take thirty children to Hill Crest, another PGL Adventure Centre near Ross on Wye, in 1990. This time there was a very muddy assault course and raft building, which demanded a team effort. Some of the children enjoyed going on a pony trek. All came home tired but happy. A group of children returned to this venue the following year and in 1992 they went to the PGL Centre near Shrewsbury.

The role of the governors increased remarkably during the early 1990s and Mr. Stephens acknowledged their valuable contribution and that of the Parents Association in his letter to *Radley News* in March 1992. He also asked local people, in a later letter, to collect Tesco's computer vouchers as the staff wanted an extra computer in the school and would need 2000 vouchers for this. The school eventually collected 1350 tokens. By combining these with those Dry Sandford School had collected, the two schools were able to obtain an Archimedes computer, which they would share. The Parents Association at this time were raising money for new playground equipment. This was fitted and a generous donation from Abingdon Lions enabled bark to be installed underneath it. Kennedy's Garden Centre at North Hinksey, Oxford, donated the turf.

The school football team - trained by teacher Dave Stemp - achieved great success in 1992 as they won the Hewlett Cup for small schools and the Herald Cup for larger schools. They also won the cluster schools' tournament. The netball team achieved good success as well. A creative arts workshop was held in the Silk Hall at Radley College for children from the cluster group. Children took part in dance, drama, singing and music workshops and the event was considered to be very successful.

Rear view of the school showing part of the playing field.

Mr. Hawes and his class made a thorough study of the history and geography of the village in May 1992. They were assisted by an archaeologist who started by making excavations in the school grounds. He chose a site where caretakers for many years had burned their rubbish and showed the children how to be responsible archaeologists. Many interesting items were found and the children had fun identifying them. Only one item of significance was discovered and that was a piece of pottery which was dated from about the 10th century. This was found at ploughing depth and, as manure had been brought in from stables around the area, its origin could not be identified.

Musical collaboration with the church took place when Mrs. Chambers' after-school singing club joined with the church choir to practise for a combined performance in Sunningwell Village Hall, about two miles from Radley.

In August 1992 the well-loved classroom assistant and former dinner lady Daphne Green retired after working for 22 years at the school.

At the beginning of the autumn term in 1992 an aerial was installed on the school roof in preparation for radio week. A ham radio was operated in Bowyer Class to 'drive' a geography topic. Radio Oxford visited the school and carried out interviews. The children made over 150 contacts in such places as New Zealand, Australia, Japan, the west coast of the USA, Alaska and South America. The results were very pleasing.

Father Keith Kinnaird, vicar of Radley from 1988 to 1995, worked closely with the children in school and church during assemblies. He linked these to the church calendar and after the service would discuss the theme with the older children.

About this time the provision of a nursery at the school was discussed.

In July 1993 Mr. Stephens took early retirement. He said in his interview for Radley History Club that the thing he was most proud of was the good grounding in all aspects of education with which children left the school. Secondary school teachers often remarked on this fact. While he was at the school, he liked the idea that he could choose his own teachers and he particularly enjoyed spending quality time with the children when he was not a teaching head. There were some extremely bright children at the school when he was there, who have gone on to be very successful in their careers, and he felt it was rewarding to think they started their education at Radley. He said that he tried to instill in children the fact that they all had different skills and abilities but they could all get kudos by trying hard.

The situation regarding the workload of head teachers changed over the years Mr. Stephens was at the school. Towards the end of his career there was far more administrative work and the fact that he had to go back to being a full-time teaching head made him decide to retire. Teaching heads often had less secretarial help than non-teaching heads, as they were in smaller schools, yet at the same time they could have similar administrative workloads. Mr. Stephens was also being expected to manage the school's financial affairs.

Chapter 9

The People 1994 - 2007

Head Teachers

Mr. David Stemp - Acting head - September 1993 - August 1994.
Mrs. Marcia Graham - September 1994 - About 1997.
Mrs. Radka Benton - September 1997 - March 2007.
Miss Frances Lockwood - April 2007 -

Assistant Teachers

Mrs. Jill Evans - September 1975 -
Mr. David Stemp. - January 1989 - August 1993.
Mrs. Janet Dix - September 1994 - August 1995.
Mrs. Jane Liddle - September 1996 - August 1997.
Katherine Rouse - ? - August 2002. September 2004 -
Mrs. Janine Beaumont - January 2000 -
Miss Mary Edmondson - September 2002 - August 2004.
Miss Elise Donnelly - September 2004 -
Mrs. Katharine McLennan -
Mrs. Maggie Morris -
Mrs. Gilson -
Mrs. Tilley - January 2002 - August 2002.
Mrs. Williams - September 1997 - September 1998.
Mrs. Pargeter - January 2002 - August 2002.
Mrs. Charalambous -
Miss Karen Linton - About April 2000 -
Mrs. Julie Ilsley - September 2004 -
Mrs. Rachel Smith - September 1998 -
Mrs. Ann Barnes - ? - August 1999.
Mrs. Luisa Penman - January 2000 - August 2003.
Miss Hope Palmer - September 2002 - August 2003.
Mrs. Susan Graney - September 2003 - August 2004.
Miss Tamsin Richards - September 2003 - August 2004.
Mrs. Capel - January 2002. - August 2002.

Learning Support/Teaching Assistants

Mrs. Saintey - ? - August 2002.
Mrs. Parkin -

Mrs. Sally Sutherland -
Mrs. Helen Summersbee -
Mrs. Claire Burton -
Louise Turner -
Debbie Emadian -
Katherine Jeffries -
Mrs. Tina McClean - 1998 -

Secretaries

Judy Woodbridge - 1995
Julie Ball - 1996 -
Mrs. Jackie Crook -

School Bursars

Mrs. Theresa Turner -

Playgroup/Pre-school Supervisor

Helen Franklin - About 1997 - August 2007.
Sara Buckley -

Playgroup/Pre-school/Foundation Assistants

Mrs. Tina McClean -
Mrs. Linzi Neale-Smith -
Mrs. Sonia Paige -
Mrs. Helen Franklin -
Mrs. Shelley Couling -
Miss Alison Grimes - ? - December 1998, January 2000 -
Carol King -
Nicolina Ellerker -
Anne Latham -

Lunch-time Supervisors

Mrs. Christina Cross -
Mrs. Sally Sutherland -
Mrs. Tina McClean - 1998 -
Mrs. Jane Hamp - ? - August 1998.

Cleaners in Charge

Mrs. Claire Burton -
Mrs. Wright -

Cleaners

Mrs. Webb - about 1976 - 1997
Mrs. Shelley Couling -
Mrs. Sue Taylor -
Mrs. Mandy Prior - 1998 -
Miss Jenny Lappage -
Mr. David Goatley -

'Lollipop' Person (School Crossing patrol)

Mrs. Jane Hamp - ? - August 1998.

Occupation not given

Mrs. Sandra Hunter - ? - August 1999.
Mr. Chris Bye - ? - August 1999.

After Mr. Stephens retired, Mr. Stemp became the acting head and the staff were Mr. Hawes, Mrs.Ward, temporarily in Mrs. Smith`s class, and Mrs. Chambers.

In February 1994 the school started on a new venture, an after-school club for children aged 5 to 12 years. It was decided that the scheme would be self-financing and run by a management committee. There would be two paid staff. In this same month the School Association became a registered charity, which helped their fund-raising efforts. The new car park in Church Road was opened and this relieved congestion outside the school at opening and closing times.

Mr. Stemp left at the end of the summer term in 1994 to study for an M.A. in education, and Mrs. Marcia Graham became the head teacher. She lived in Abingdon but had been teaching in South Oxfordshire prior to commencing at Radley.

Nick Hawes, the teacher of the top junior children at the school, wrote in the *Radley News* in March 1995 about the work the children were doing with their pond. They had created a wildlife meadow, a rotting log pile, bird tables and bird boxes, a squirrel run and food store, a hedgehog home, a newt and frog rockery and a butterfly border and plant area. John Ward and a working party helped one Saturday morning to clear the pond and it was then considered to be in a healthy condition. In fact, Long Wittenham Nature Reserve officials stated that it was one of the best natural pond areas left in the county and should be protected. In 1997 the school won fourth prize in a competition sponsored by Rover, the motor car manufacturer, for their development work around the pond.

Jenny Beauchamp, Rachel Smith, Kevin Wood and Lisa Wood brought honour to the school when they won third place in the county round of the First Aid Challenge.

In 1995 the School Association were working towards providing maths resources for the school, particularly for the infants' classroom.

At the end of the summer term in 1995 the school said goodbye to Mrs. Lacey, who had been the cleaner in charge for 17 years. In 1997, Mrs. Webb, a cleaner at the school for 21 years, also retired.

There was a new venture beginning after the summer holidays when 'Bramleys', a Montessori-style nursery and an after-school care facility, opened in the school grounds.

At the beginning of 1996 there were 69 children on roll and a new secretary, Julie Ball, joined the school. School meals were being brought from St. Swithun's School in Kennington. The vicar was the Rev. Thomas Patrick Gibbons (1996 - 2004). When he left, he was replaced by the Rev. Pamela Joyce McKellen.

The start of 1996 saw much industrious activity. Clubs had started in football, art, recorder, dance and French. Visits were planned to the local area and a museum. Korky Paul, the book illustrator, visited the school in connection with 'Book Week'. In mid-March the older juniors accompanied Mr. Hawes on a PGL Adventure weekend in Wales. The School Association was busy raising money for another computer but had to disband the 120 Club for lack of support. The National Lottery had arrived to compete against it and there were fewer children in school and consequently fewer parents. The aim of the Association that year was to have two computers in each of the three classrooms.

For many years there seemed to be no inspection of schools. Organisers came from the LEA to assist teachers. This all changed with the new style of inspection, which the Government introduced, called Ofsted (Office for Standards in Education) inspections. Mrs. Graham remarked that it was heavy going when the number of inspectors matched the number of teachers. The result, though, was that the school was 'on the up'. The report congratulated the school on the caring ethos, the good behaviour of the pupils and the school's positive Christian ethos. The inspectors felt that there was good teaching in all the classes and some of the teaching was of a very high standard. The children were highly motivated and the parents very supportive.

In December 1996 the first approaches by the playgroup committee requesting the use of Bowyer classroom were made. There was worry that it would cost too much but the committee were hoping that grants and donations might help. It was worked out that it would cost about £9000 to refurbish the room and provide toilet and kitchen facilities. Fund raising had to start in earnest. At that time the playgroup used the new village hall, which had been built to replace the old, now demolished, hall in Lower Radley. The playgroup moved into the school in the autumn term of 1997, having raised £15,000 for the necessary changes. The new room was officially opened by Patrick (Paddy) Dockar-Drysdale on 7 February 1998. A lot of volunteer labour was used, especially in the decoration of the room. The group became known as Radley Pre-School in April 1998 and was open to children aged two and a half years to school age on a part-time basis. The staff found the new accommodation much more satisfactory as they no longer had to put all the equipment away each night or deal with the effects of a previous night's party, by a third party user, as they had done in the village hall. In April 1997 nursery vouchers were introduced and finances were helped by this. A week after their official opening the pre-school had an Ofsted inspection with a very positive result. In Spring 1999 they had another inspection and again encouraging comments were made.

Mrs. Graham gave in her resignation for March 1997 as she thought she was leaving the country with her family. Mrs. Radka Benton was appointed in her place. However, the best-laid plans failed to materialise and Mrs. Graham found herself as acting head at Thameside School in Abingdon.

When Mrs. Benton started, she was teaching for four days each week but was able to have cover for one day to work in the office. At the end of 1997 Mr. Nick Hawes left the school to take up a position in Suffolk.

During 1998 David Beckett, as director of music at Radley Church, started a school choir, which participated in the 'Festival of Voices' performance at Dorchester Abbey. Choirs from schools in the local area came together to take part in this.

About 1999 the school again started asking parents to collect Tesco computer vouchers and Walker's free book tokens as they would help to buy necessary books and equipment for the school. A summer 'fayre' was held and the children had their own stall to raise money for Kosovan refugees. Money was also raised by organising a sponsored walk.

1999 was the first year that Year 6 had to do SATs. There were three tests for English, three for maths, and two for science.

To celebrate the new millennium all the school-age children in Radley were given a commemorative mug. These were presented by David Buckle, chairman of Radley Parish Council, at a ceremony in the school. The children contributed to the millennium time capsule and were there with a number of villagers to see it buried in Radley's new graveyard.

The Pre-School was on television in early 2000 illustrating an excellent example of the type of relaxed and informal setting in which children aged four could learn through play as recommended by the Government's Select Committee.

In 2000 a group of children belonging to the school's media club won an award for an animated film about the school, using clay models. The *Oxford Times* article, which informed the public about the award, also mentioned that Mr. Ian Davenport of Radley College had raised £3500 through sponsorship towards new computers for the school. He had taken part in a gruelling 24-hour challenge climbing the Lake District peaks because some of the boys in his house at the College helped once a week at the school.

The idea of an after-school club once again was put forward and an article was written in *Radley News* asking how many parents would be interested in such a service.

In 2000 there was an Ofsted inspection. The school, which the inspectors considered to be an improving school, had about 60 pupils in three classes. Following the inspection the *Oxford Mail* reported:

> The school has won praise for the quality of its teaching and pupil behaviour. Teaching at the school was rated as 100% satisfactory with 60% of lessons good or better.
>
> The children had very good attitudes, behaviour and relationships and were courteous and friendly.
>
> New literacy and numeracy strategies are being used to improve pupil attainment.
>
> The excellent partnership between the school and the parents was a good feature, together with the enthusiastic support of the parents in the life of the school.

Improvements are needed particularly in the areas of science and ICT (Information and communications technology). Governors have promised these will form a key part of the school's action plan for the future, along with an ongoing drive to improve standards and attainment

In another report, from the National Society, the school was praised for its strong Christian ethos in which all pupils and staff were valued, cared and nurtured. The inspector also praised the importance placed on pupil voices.

Parents and friends were a considerable help to the school. Radley Quilters helped the children to produce a millennium quilt and Ron Starkey ran an after-school gardening club, which is now being run by Maureen and Derek Cook. Boys from Radley College helped in the classroom and with repairs and manual work around the school. For many years Dot Hewlett has sold 'Webb Ivory' cards and raised money for the school and other charities. Dot's involvement with the school began when her children started there in 1965. Two years later Miss Cross encouraged Dot to train as a teacher, which she was able to do. While she was training she visited the school to research the historical documents for a paper on the history of education. On qualifying, Dot became a teacher in schools around Abingdon and after retiring she was a supply teacher for Radley School for about two years.

Four children left the school to go to Fitzharrys Comprehensive School, in Abingdon, in July 2000. Before they left, they were each presented with a dictionary at a service in the church on the last day of term. This was followed by a family barbeque in the evening.

At the end of 2000 the children in Thames Class visited Christ Church Cathedral, in Oxford, as part of their project on pilgrimages. They dressed as pilgrims and pretended to return to the 13th century by coming to the Cathedral to pray and to present gifts. Cherwell and Isis class had a visit from Abingdon Fire Service.

In 2001 the children in Thames Class, who were eight years old or older, gave an outdoor performance of a specially adapted version of *A Midsummer Night's Dream*. The teacher, Katherine Rouse, felt it was a good introduction to Shakespeare and to acting.

There was an after-school club called 'Rascals' in operation in 2001. It ran every day until 5.30 p.m.

The surface under the outside playground equipment was changed from wood chips to an all weather safety surface in early 2001. The money for it was raised by the School Association.

In 2001 there was a restructuring of the classes and a new reception class, called the Foundation Unit, was created. This was for children who would become five years old during the term they started their schooling.

Following proposals and consultations with the LEA in 2002, the school was given joint foundation partnership with the pre-school.

There was another inspection by Ofsted in November 2002 and the school was deemed 'satisfactory'. The new foundation unit, the pupils' attitudes and behaviour and the parental and community contributions to the school were all commended. There was work for the governors to do but many of the suggestions contained in the report had already been identified and the school had started implementing them.

The letter written in *Radley News* by the head teacher, Radka Benton, in June 2003 invited the villagers to visit the new features in the school grounds. These were two beautiful living willow structures, a working allotment and the millennium garden.

Following the conversion of the kitchen area to a new classroom, the school set its sights on converting the old building for disabled access. Computers were gradually being transferred to broadband connections and parents were encouraged to contact the school through email.

In November 2003 the pre-school and the foundation class became a joint unit under the combined name of Radley Partnership Foundation Unit. The foundation partnership received another Ofsted inspection in 2004. The inspectors deemed the day care 'good' and the nursery education 'high quality'. The staff were highly praised.

A new scheme was introduced by the Government at the beginning of 2005 whereby every child aged seven years or under would be entitled to a piece of fresh fruit or vegetable every day. Radley School made sure the children had this.

Fund raising continued throughout all the more recent years and in 2005, in one evening, £4000 was raised at Radley College. The event began with a drinks reception, followed by a three-course meal and dancing to Will Matthew's band. Radley College donated the venue and all money went towards the Radley Partnership Foundation Unit for a new building. In the same year the spring fair at the school raised over £1000 and with this money a new computer was bought for Isis classroom, playground picnic benches were replaced, a subsidy was given towards the whole school outing in July and stylish new desks were provided for Thames class.

The Ofsted inspectors visited the school in September 2006. There were then 85 children on roll aged between 4 and 11. The following is part of the overall effectiveness report issued by the inspectors:

> Radley Church of England Primary School provides a satisfactory quality of education and has strengths in its curriculum and in the way it cares, guides and supports its pupils. This promotes good personal development and pupils show positive attitudes to learning. Its good links with other agencies are used effectively to provide specialist help where it is needed. Parents greatly appreciate all that the school does, expressing the view that all the staff have the interests of the children at heart. The head teacher is supported well by the staff and governors. The effective provision in the foundation stage gives the children a good start to their academic and personal development. The school's strong focus on the individual encourages the pupils to behave well and take on responsibilities very willingly.

The diocesan report of November 6th 2006 was equally pleasing. It stated that:

> Radley Church of England Primary School provides a distinctive Christian environment where children feel safe, are nurtured and valued. The children have a positive attitude to learning and behaviour and take on responsibilities willingly.

By early 2007 the school had its own web site and is able now to communicate with the wider community through this.

Mrs. Benton decided to retire in 2007 and Miss Frances Lockwood became, after the Easter holiday, the new head teacher.

Chapter 10

Conclusion

Radley Church of England School has been part of the village for more than 150 years and has seen many changes during that time. It has had good and not so good times and is typical of many rural schools.

In the very early days of the school, the children came almost exclusively from the families of agricultural workers. Life was hard for these people in their little tied cottages, often up to a mile away from the school. There was no running water, no gas, no electricity, no transport and very little money to be had to feed, pay for schooling and clothe the large families which were the norm. Most of the families were related to one another by birth or marriage and there was a strong sense of family loyalty. Children of primary school age were needed at home to look after younger siblings or to help their parents working on the local farms. Absenteeism and the late arrival of the children were the bane of the teachers' lives. The seasons and seasonal epidemics played an important role in whether the children attended school or not. Inspectors sometimes struggled to find something good to say about the school in the early times, but the teachers deserved a lot of sympathy when their difficulties were taken into consideration.

Gradually families were prepared to sacrifice the help of their children to ensure they had a good education and the numbers who thought like that increased with time as the value of being able to read and write was recognised. When compulsory school attendance was introduced and a more exciting curriculum was taught, the school showed a tremendous improvement. Certain head teachers and teachers stood out as being very successful and the inspectors were able to give praise in their reports.

As transport became more accessible, especially with the coming of the railway to the village, families started to be more mobile. Fewer people worked on the land as farming became more mechanized and industry offered other opportunities for employment. This resulted in a gradual movement of people away from the village. At the same time new residents, who often worked in surrounding towns, were coming in. New houses were built and caravan parks appeared, increasing the size of the village and changing the school population. There are still a few children at the school who are descended from Radley's earlier inhabitants but the majority of children now come from families who are relatively new to the area.

The original 1873 building continues to be used and externally it looks very similar to what it was like all those years ago. The contents are very different though. Computers now line the walls where the old desks once stood and these, together with a well-equipped reference library, enable children to have access to a world children of 150 years ago could never even have dreamt of or imagined.

Radley Primary School continues to grow and with the new building about to be built, an excellent staff, supportive parents, governors and friends, together with children eager to learn, the future looks very positive.

Radley School in the winter of 2007.

Mission statement of the School 2008.

Radley Church of England Primary School
aims for every child to achieve success to the best of their
ability in a welcoming centre of learning.

Christian values, principles and standards lie at the heart of
our education.

Our school will be a place where every child is valued and their
individuality and achievements celebrated.

All children regardless of differences in race, gender and faith
will be respected and encouraged to become responsible global
citizens.

Children will be encouraged to develop positive reflective
attitudes that lead to high personal and academic standards.

Our positive approach to behaviour will ensure that all children
are given the opportunity to work and play in a calm, safe
environment.

An atmosphere of openness, trust and respect will be
encouraged between children, their parents and the wider
school community to foster good communications to the
benefit of the children's education.

We create a stimulating, learning environment that nurtures
curiosity, enthusiasm, awareness and industry.

A Brief Summary of the History of Education in England.

The Radley Church of England School story has been closely tied to the history of education in England and the following is a guide to help to relate the various government initiatives to the school

1811. The National Society for Promoting the Education of the Poor in the Principles of the Established Church was set up by the Church of England to provide schools.

1833. The Government allocated a grant of £20,000 towards erecting Church of England schools, provided that at least half of the cost of the building had been raised by private subscription. This was the first time that the Government had been involved with education in England and Wales.

1839. A Committee of the Queen's Privy Council was charged with overseeing elementary education and granting aid to voluntary schools. School inspectors were appointed. This committee carried out its work through an Education Department, which existed until it was replaced by the Board of Education in 1899.

1841. School Sites Act. This Act, the culmination of several smaller Acts, empowered owners of land to make sites, not exceeding one acre, available for schools in the education of poor persons or for the residence of a school master or mistress. A reversion clause provided for such land to revert to the original owner or his successors if it ceased to be used for the purposes of the Act. The land could be vested in the minister (e.g. vicar) and churchwardens of the parish.

1844. School Sites Act. This Act set out the terms and conditions upon which Parliamentary grants would be made to schools, including inspection by Her Majesty's Inspectors.

1870. Elementary Education Act (Forsters Act). This was the first major Education Act. A driving force behind it was the need for Britain to remain competitive in world commerce and also because working class children would now grow up to be voters and the Government did not want them voting the wrong way. The Reform Act 1867 meant that all men aged over 21 who lived in a borough with an address could vote. This brought a small proportion of working class men into the system for the first time. It was 1918 before all men, and women over the age of 30, could vote. Forster's Act 1870 attempted to provide elementary education for all children up to 10 years of age. It allowed School Boards, elected by the ratepayers, to be set up to provide primary education in areas where the existing provision was insufficient. The Boards were financed by a precept on the local Poor Law rate and they could build schools and compel attendance for children aged 5 to 12, but many Boards did not use this power. Fees of a few pennies a week were charged to parents but the Boards paid the fees of poor children, even if they attended Church of England schools. All schools were to be inspected and individual schools continued to be eligible for an annual government grant on the basis of the inspection reports.

1876. Elementary Education Act (Sandon's Act). This Act placed a duty on parents to ensure that their children received elementary instruction in reading, writing and arithmetic. School Attendance Committees were set up, for areas where there were no School Boards, to compel attendance.

1880. Elementary Education Act (Mundella's Act). This extended the provisions of the 1876 Act regarding compulsory school attendance for children aged from 5 to 10 years. For poorer families this proved difficult because of the temptation to send them to work to earn extra pennies for the family. Attendance Officers often visited the homes of children who failed to attend school. Children under the age of 13 who were employed were required to have a certificate to show that they had reached the necessary educational standard before leaving school and if the employer could not show the certificate he was penalised.

1891. Elementary Education Act. This made grants available to all schools to enable them to cease charging for basic elementary education.

1893. Elementary Education (School Attendance) Act. The school leaving age was raised to 11 years. Another Act in the same year, entitled the Elementary Education (Blind and Deaf Children) Act, enabled the provision of special schools for a group who previously had no access to an official education.

1897. The Voluntary Schools Act provided for government grants to be paid to public elementary schools not funded by School Boards (e.g. church schools).

1899. Elementary Education (School Attendance) Act (1893) Amendment Act. The school leaving age was raised to 12.

1899. Board of Education Act. This set up a Board of Education in 1900 which became responsible for education policy in England and Wales, taking over the duties of the Education Department which had existed since 1839. The Board was succeeded by a Ministry of Education in 1944. There have been several changes since and the Department for Children, Schools and Families is the present body (2007).

1902. Education Act (Balfour's Act). County Councils were created in 1889 under the provisions of the Local Government Act 1888 and took on much of the work previously performed by *ad hoc* bodies. Balfour's Act abolished the school boards set up under the Elementary Education Act 1870 and transferred their duties to the Local Education Authorities (LEAs) of the County Councils and County Borough Councils. It also brought voluntary schools (such as Church of England schools) under some government control through provision of funding through the local rates. Four managers were appointed by the school and two by the LEA.

1918. Education Act (Fisher's Act). Education became compulsory for children from 5 to 14 years of age. Also included was provision for ancillary services, such as medical inspections, nursery schools and centres for children with special needs. The Act did not come into force until the Education Act 1921.

1944. Education Act (Butler's Act). This Act, because of the effects of World War II, did not come into force until April 1947. It raised the school-leaving age to 15 and established the tripartite system of secondary education by creating grammar, technical and secondary modern schools and allowed for the foundation of comprehensive schools to combine all three strands. A division, which many LEAs had already adopted, was made between primary education (5 to 11 years old) and secondary education (11 to 15 years old). All education was free. The 11-plus examination was introduced, which was intended to assess the type of secondary school most suitable for the pupil's abilities and aptitudes. Church schools could opt into the maintained system by choosing between aided and controlled status. In an Aided Church of England school, church involvement was very much to the fore. The church authorities retained ownership of the school land and buildings. They were responsible for repairing the buildings and for building extensions, receiving a percentage of the cost from the Local Education Authority. They nominated the majority of governors, who employed the staff and set the admissions procedure. In a Controlled Church of England school, the Local Education Authority ran the school, employed the staff and set the admission criteria. The school land and buildings remained vested in the church authorities but repairs and extensions were the responsibility of the LEA, with contributions from the governing body, a minority of members of which were chosen by the church authorities. The Board of Education, which had been created in 1899, was renamed the Ministry of Education. A provision to raise the school-leaving age to 16 was not implemented until 1973.

1950s. Middle schools were introduced in a few areas of the country, e.g. Leicestershire and Oxford, which bridged the gap between primary and secondary schools. These have now been almost completely phased out.

1972. Education Act. The school-leaving age was raised to 16 from 1st September 1973.

1973. Education (Work Experience) Act. This allowed LEAs to organise work experience for the final-year school pupils.

1988. Education Reform Act. By virtue of this Act schools had to compete with each other for pupils, on the theory that the bad schools would lose pupils to the good ones, forcing the bad schools to improve or be closed down. Other innovations introduced by the Act were:

- The National Curriculum, requiring schools to teach certain subjects and syllabuses.
- National assessments at the Key Stages 1 - 4, Ages 7, 11, 14 and 16.
- Standard Assessment Tests (SATs) to be given at Key Stages 1-3, but the GCSE would be used for Key Stage 4.
- League Tables (published) to show a school's performance.
- Formula funding, which meant that the more pupils a school could attract, the more money it got.
- Open enrolment, giving parents a choice of schools.
- A provision for a school to opt out of local government control if enough parents agreed.

1996. Education Act. This was a consolidating act, re-enacting the provisions of several smaller Acts, which were then repealed. It set the school leaving date as the last Friday in June in the school year in which the child reaches the age of 16.

1997 onwards has seen several further changes and these include the literacy and numeracy hours in primary schools, target setting and a maximum class size of 30 for infant children.

Index of Surnames

165